The Art of Scouting

The Art of Scouting

How the Hockey Experts Really Watch the Game and Decide Who Makes It

SHANE MALLOY

FOREWORD BY BRIAN BURKE
General Manager, Toronto Maple Leafs

John Wiley & Sons Canada, Ltd.

Library and Archives Canada Cataloguing in Publication Data

Malloy, Shane, 1972–
    The art of scouting: how the hockey experts really watch the game and decide who makes it / Shane Malloy.

Includes index.
ISBN 978-0-470-68150-3

    1. Hockey–Scouting. 2. Hockey scouts. 3. Hockey players. 4. Minor league hockey. 5. National Hockey League. I. Title.

GV847.M4654 2011   796.962'62   C2010-906938-2

ISBN 978-0-470-96345-6 (e-PDF); 978-0-470-96347-0 (e-Mobi); 978-0-470-96346-3 (e-PUB)

Production Credits
Cover design: Adrian So
Front cover photo credit: ©iStockphoto.com/jgareri
Back cover photo credit: ©iStockphoto.com/Thinkstock
Interior text design: Natalia Burobina
Typesetter: Laserwords
Printer: Friesens

John Wiley & Sons Canada, Ltd.
6045 Freemont Blvd.
Mississauga, Ontario
L5R 4J3

Printed in Canada

1 2 3 4 5 FP 15 14 13 12 11

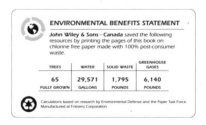

ENVIRONMENTAL BENEFITS STATEMENT
John Wiley & Sons - Canada saved the following resources by printing the pages of this book on chlorine free paper made with 100% post-consumer waste.

TREES	WATER	SOLID WASTE	GREENHOUSE GASES
65	29,571	1,795	6,140
FULLY GROWN	GALLONS	POUNDS	POUNDS

Calculations based on research by Environmental Defense and the Paper Task Force. Manufactured at Friesens Corporation

To my grandfather Buddy Malloy.

"Scouting sucks," he said emphatically. "Go to the wrong door and the guy won't let you in the rink because you don't have the right ID . . . Missed the train back . . . Try to find a hotel. All that type of screwy stuff. Whatever those guys make they ought to get a raise because it sucks."

Ken Hitchock,
Stanley Cup Winning NHL Coach

Contents

Foreword

By Brian Burke

The lifeblood of the National Hockey League is scouting, and its largely invisible army of unsung heroes consists of seven hundred or so full- and part-time scouts, both amateur and professional.

Here's an ad for a scouting position: "Wanted: NHL Amateur Scout. Need a keen eye for projecting how players who are seventeen will play when they are twenty-five years old in the best league in the world. Pay only fair, hours long, travel brutal. Bushels of criticism and scorn from the media when you're wrong. Faint praise when you're right. Multiple relocations likely over your career." An ad for a professional scout wouldn't be much different.

The Art of Scouting peels away the layers involved in securing players on your NHL roster. You have to find them, then draft them, then develop them into NHL players. Shane Malloy goes into great detail on the problem of unearthing players and getting them to the show. The information is accurate and interesting. But what makes this book fascinating is the overlay of expert commentary from the team personnel themselves. Every tale the author tells, every process he describes, is buttressed by commentary from the troops in the field, veteran insiders with savvy, know-how and a proven history of success.

The Art of Scouting is a book that every hockey fan will want to read. For the serious fan, and especially for the young man or woman who hopes to work in the field, this is a must-read.

Shane Malloy is no stranger to the business of hockey and no novice when it comes to writing about hockey prospects.

A donation from the proceeds of this book will go to the Brendan Burke Memorial Internship to assist college graduates pursuing a career in hockey operations.

BRENDAN BURKE MEMORIAL INTERNSHIP

The annual 12-month internship was recently announced and is intended for a recent college graduate interested in hockey operations as a career. The internship has been established in memory of the late Brendan Burke, who passed away unexpectedly on February 5, 2010, at age 21. Brendan, the son of Brian Burke, general manager of the 2010 U.S. Olympic Men's Ice Hockey Team, was a student at Miami University and served as a hockey operations assistant with Miami's men's ice hockey team.

USA Hockey Foundation

Brendan Burke Memorial Internship
   1775 Bob Johnson Drive
   Colorado Springs, CO 80906
   www.USAHockey.com

Miami University

Brendan Burke Memorial Scholarship
   Office of Development
   725 East Chestnut Street
   Oxford, OH 45056-2480
   www.forloveandhonor.org

Preface

Like those of most Canadian boys, my dreams of becoming an NHL player faded away as reality set in, but my passion for the game remains as vibrant as ever. I was fortunate to have a grandfather who was not only a player and a fan of hockey but also a student of the game. We would spend countless hours glued to the television set, watching game after game. Often our excitement (and, occasionally, our frustration) led to hypothetical questions, such as, "If you were the general manager or coach, what would you do?"

Watching the games on TV was one thing, but going to real live NHL games was the greatest thing ever. I distinctly remember my first NHL game. It was December 16, 1979, and the Edmonton Oilers faced the Winnipeg Jets at the Northlands Coliseum. To this day, the sounds and smells of that game still flash by every time I walk into an arena. We walked through the concourse, and the air crackled with the energy and excitement of the fans. I was seven years old, and I beamed as my grandfather bought me a Wayne Gretzky sweater. In awe, I kept staring down at the new Oilers crest on my chest, heedlessly bumping into people along the way. Having that hockey sweater and a ticket to the game felt like being given the password to a secret club.

The hallway from the concourse to the stands of the Northlands Coliseum was narrow and dark as I shuffled behind my grandfather. When we stepped from it into the brightly lit arena to take our seats, I stopped and stared in utter amazement at the grandeur of it all. And at that moment, I was hooked for life. My grandfather said he had never seen anyone smile so big in his life, he thought my smile was going to split my head in two. The game ended (a 9-2 victory for the Oilers), but the magic never did.

Even as a kid I was interested in what went on behind the scenes—who was making the trades and who was drafting the next big star. I recall sitting at the kitchen table with a couple of notebooks, a newspaper full of the latest stats, and a pile of hockey cards all spread out in front of me. I was busy trying to figure out which players would get traded where and why. I would scribble down potential trades and explain them in as much detail as a 10-year-old kid can come up with. So I guess you could say I've always been a Draftnik, fascinated by the process of discovering new talent and building an organization from the ground up—it's almost better than the game itself. In the beginning I was like most people, thinking, "How hard can it be to pick out the best player on the ice?" But after doing some research, I quickly realized that the most skilled players in a junior or college hockey game are not necessarily the most suited for the NHL. It became evident to me that scouting is not an exact science, but a learned skill based on science, art, and intuition.

After realizing that my initial thoughts on scouting were wrong, I stepped back and re-evaluated. Finding the answer to "How does a scout know who is a potential NHL player?" became a quest. At first I thought I could get the insight from fellow members of the media, but even the veterans were just as in the dark as I was. To satisfy my curiosity, it made sense to go directly to the source: the scouts themselves. But much to my dismay, the scouts were unwilling to simply give away their trade secrets. In the world of scouting, information on the process and the players is a commodity worth more than gold.

At this point I had a dilemma: I had questions and the only people who had the answers were not sharing. So I asked Craig Button, at the time General Manager of the Calgary Flames, his thoughts on the matter, and he said, "The best way to understand scouting is to pay your dues and learn to scout." He told me to go to as many games as I could, to sit in the corner of the rink, and to take notes on what I saw. He advised me to make a list of skills I thought were important and to use that as a guide, to keep an open mind, to not rush to judgement, and to ask questions.

Following his advice, I immersed myself in the scouting industry and the development of players. It took a long time to understand what to look for, as the ability to break down players' skills is not an easy task. The difficulty is compounded by the need to project players' potential into the future to determine if they have what it takes to make it at the next level. I discovered the role of scout is multi-faceted—they're expected to be Nostradamus, Sigmund Freud, Dick Tracy, and James Bond all rolled into one.

I was lucky enough to have Paddy Ginnell and Lorne Davis tell me some of the little rules of the scouting fraternity, which helped me become accepted as a peer. House rules include: never ask a scout about his list for the upcoming Draft, demonstrate your work ethic and commitment by being at every game you can, stand by your opinion and be able to back it up, be fair in your player assessments, and most importantly, treat everyone with courtesy and respect regardless of their position.

Armed with their tips, I spent a decade learning the craft of scouting and interviewing countless scouts. Then I decided to use what I'd learned to create *The Art of Scouting*. Have you ever wondered how an NHL scout decides which teenager will become an NHL player five years down the road? Well, you're not alone; fans and even hockey insiders have asked this question for generations, and this book will help to answer it. *The Art of Scouting* is for any hockey fan who ever wondered about the how and why of the secret world of scouting hockey. You'll get a peek inside the fascinating world of scouting, understand the impact that scouts have on the quality of the game, appreciate how tough their job is, and learn how they make their evaluations.

Perhaps the most important thing I've learned after attending over 1,500 games is that you can't claim to know it all. Not a day goes by when you don't learn something new. In the spirit of always learning, I've created a companion website (www.artofscouting.com) that will have updates, more information, and discussions for both diehard Draftniks and those who have just caught the scouting bug.

Acknowledgements

Anytime someone decides to put pen to paper, the words become like a living, breathing entity that cannot continue to survive without the love and support of many people. I have been blessed with the loving support of my fiancée, Tanya, whose patience is unrivalled. The enthusiasm of my family and friends helped make this book fun to write, and I will always appreciate their support. Without Arnold and Rose Steiner and their family, I know my life would have been drastically different and this book would always have remained a dream.

Special thanks go to Mel Schmidt who assisted me in transcribing many interviews during the last few months. Her hyper devotion and love affair with Pierre McGuire's voice always made me laugh, and I owe her a debt of gratitude. Thanks to my editor and trusted friend Chris McCluskey, who is perhaps the most underrated hockey writer on the planet. To my literary agent Leigh Augustine who took care of the details and made things easy for me. To Karen Milner, my executive editor at John Wiley & Sons who believed in and championed this project from day one, and my editor, Diana Byron, I can never say thank you enough.

This foray into the world of hockey scouting began over a decade ago when I started writing a prospect column for FOX Sports. At the time, there were very few hockey media outlets that had any interest in discussing the next generation of players on a regular basis. Fortunately for me, Scott Wilson, the hockey editor at FOX Sports, gave me an opportunity to explore this unique aspect of the game. I asked a fine group of up-and-coming writers to contribute with me, and if it were not for the hard work of Eugene Belashchenko, Brad Coccimiglio, Chris McCluskey, Jason Shaner, Craig Stancher, and Adam Wodon, the discussion of prospects never would have had the success it has. I would be remiss if I didn't mention the fact that I was fortunate enough to sit beside Eric Duhatschek and Kelly Hrudey in the press box; their advice and mentorship helped steer me around many landmines.

From a scouting perspective, I was also very fortunate to sit down beside Paddy Ginnell and Lorne Davis, two veteran NHL scouts who introduced me to scouting. Both gentlemen were gracious with their time and gave me the initial tools I needed to learn the trade and form my own opinions. I was also lucky to meet Craig Button, who at the time was the Calgary Flames general manager. Despite how busy he was on a day-to-day basis, he always took the time to answer any questions I had and made me feel like a peer. I am compelled to mention three current NHL scouts—Glen Dirk, Bruce Haralson, and Tim Burke—who have helped me understand the business and history of scouting. The dedication they have to their profession and the respect they show to their peers make them stewards of the game.

At the 2003 NHL Entry Draft, I was a guest on an Internet radio show hosted by Russ Cohen on the Sportsology Radio Network. This turned into a co-hosting gig with Russ for *The NHL Hour*, also on the Sportsology Radio Network. Little did I realize that one radio spot would introduce me to one of my best friends and open up a whole new world of broadcasting. It also led to our *Hockey Prospect* show and the *Business of Hockey* show on XM Home Ice, where we can still be heard today. If not for Russ's unwavering support and belief in me over the past eight years, most of my projects would not have seen the light of day.

A special thanks goes to the many members of the media who have helped me along the way, for no apparent reason other than I must have looked like I really needed it. All these people have made a tremendous difference: Eugene Belashchenko, Darren Dreger, Jonathan Gilhen, Randy Gorman, Louie Jean, Chris Johnston, Gus Katsaros, Patrick King, Peter Loubardias, Bob McKenzie, Rick Quinton, Dan Russell, Matt Sekeras, Colin Tiggelaar, Daniel Tolensky, Stu Walters, and Jonathan West. To everyone over at XM Home Ice who stuck with us during the initial stages of our show—we owe you all beers. In particular, thanks to Joe Thistle, the program director at XM Home Ice, who stood by us and saw the value of the content and gave us tremendous creative leeway. The online web producers at Rogers Sportsnet and TSN who had to edit my ramblings in the past are some of my favourite people. Thanks also to both Phil Coffey and Shawn Roarke at NHL.com who gave me an opportunity to provide prospect content to a mass audience when very few saw its importance.

To the guys at Ramp Management and Ramp Interactive—Edmund Chu, Brendan Kenny, Brad Kronewitt, Marc Kronewitt, and Marshall Kronewitt: your guidance and support have been nothing short of amazing. Thanks to all the player agents who take my calls and give me their time and professionalism, and who take more public grief than they deserve. One player agent in particular I would like to thank is Kurt Overhardt, who has become a trusted confidant.

This book never would have been transformed into reality without the help of the public relations departments at the NHL, AHL, CHL, USHL, Hockey Canada, USA Hockey, and IIHF. You have my constant appreciation and gratitude for hunting down people and making them available to me. Three individuals at the NHL office who I must make a special note of are Mark Fischel, Dave McCarthy, and Julie Young, who always take care of both Russ Cohen and I. My eternal gratitude goes out to the Calgary Flames' Peter Hanlon and Sean O'Brien, as they gave me my first media credentials to the NHL and that opened the door.

Finally, to the fraternity of scouts who contributed to this book, and to all of them who made me feel like one of the guys, my respect for you cannot be measured. There is a list of scouting and NHL personnel, past and present, that I must acknowledge. It was their direct contribution not only to this project but also as my mentors in learning to scout that made all of this possible. I will always be in debt to Tim Burke, Doug Wilson, and the entire San Jose Sharks scouting staff for allowing me to sit in on their NHL Draft player meetings.

CONTRIBUTORS

Mike Antonovich, Amateur Scout (St. Louis Blues)

Mike Barnett, Director of U.S. Amateur Scouting (New York Rangers)

Marc Bergevin, Director of Player Personnel (Chicago Blackhawks)

Tim Bernhardt, Director of Amateur Scouting (Dallas Stars)

Craig Billington, Assistant General Manager (Colorado Avalanche)

Scott Bradley, Director of Player Personnel (Boston Bruins)

Bob Brown, Amateur Scout (Edmonton Oilers)

Brian Burke, General Manager (Toronto Maple Leafs)

Tim Burke, Director of Scouting (San Jose Sharks)

Craig Button, NHL Network Analyst and Former NHL General Manager

Tod Button, Director of Scouting (Calgary Flames)

Paul Castron, Director of Amateur Scouting (Columbus Blue Jackets)

Gordie Clark, Director of Player Personnel (New York Rangers)

Glen Cochrane, Amateur Scout (Anaheim Ducks)

Marcel Comeau, Head Scout (Atlanta Thrashers)

Dave Conte, VP of Hockey Operations, Director of Scouting (New Jersey Devils)

Jeff Crisp, Amateur Scout (Anaheim Ducks)

Brad Davis, Amateur Scout (Edmonton Oilers)

Craig Demetrick, Amateur Scout (Florida Panthers)

Glen Dirk, Amateur Scout (New Jersey Devils)

Rick Dudley, General Manager (Atlanta Thrashers)

John Ferguson Jr., Director of Pro Scouting (San Jose Sharks)

Brent Flahr, Assistant General Manager (Minnesota Wild)

Cliff Fletcher, Legendary Former NHL General Manager

Emile Francis, Legendary Former NHL General Manager, Scout, and Player

Pat Funk, Amateur Scout (San Jose Sharks)

Mike Futa, Co-Director of Amateur Scouting (Los Angeles Kings)

Ernie Gare, Amateur Scout (New York Rangers)

Laurence Gilman, Assistant General Manager (Vancouver Canucks)

Dan Ginnell, Amateur Scout (St. Louis Blues)

Erin Ginnell, Amateur Scout (Florida Panthers)

Jeff Gorton, Assistant Director of Player Personnel (New York Rangers)

Keith Gretzky, Director of Amateur Scouting (Phoenix Coyotes)

Brian Gross, Amateur Scout (San Jose Sharks)

Jim Hammett, NHL Scout

Bruce Haralson, Pro Scout (Detroit Red Wings)

Jay Heinbuck, Director of Amateur Scouting (Pittsburgh Penguins)

Paul Henry, Hockey Consultant and Former NHL Scout

Corey Hirsch, Goalie Scout (St. Louis Blues)

Charlie Hodge, Amateur Scout (Tampa Bay Lightning)

Dennis Holland, Amateur Scout (Dallas Stars)

Paul Holmgren, General Manager (Philadelphia Flyers)

Ryan Jankowski, Amateur Scout (Montreal Canadiens)

Al Jensen, NHL Central Scouting

Marshall Johnston, Director of Professional Scouting (Carolina Hurricanes)

Vaughn Karpan, Pro Scout (Montreal Canadiens)

Jeff Kealtey, Chief Amateur Scout (Nashville Predators)

Jarmo Kekalainen, General Manager (Jokerit Helsinki)

Mark Kelley, Director of Amateur Scouting (Chicago Blackhawks)

Tim Keon, Amateur Scout (Chicago Blackhawks)

Rick Knickle, Amateur Scout (Nashville Predators)

Tom Kurvers, Assistant General Manager (Tampa Bay Lightning)

Rick Lanz, Amateur Scout (Colorado Avalanche)

Scott Luce, Director of Amateur Scouting (Florida Panthers)

Tony MacDonald, Director of Amateur Scouting (Carolina Hurricanes)

Stu MacGregor, Director of Amateur Scouting (Edmonton Oilers)

Ross Mahoney, Director of Amateur Scouting (Washington Capitals)

Garth Malarchuk, Amateur Scout (Toronto Maple Leafs)

Dean Malkoc, Amateur Scout (Boston Bruins)

E.J. McGuire, Director (NHL Central Scouting)

Pierre McGuire, TSN Analyst and Former NHL Coach and Scout

Ernie "Punch" McLean, Legendary WHL Coach

Tom McVie, Pro Scout (Boston Bruins)

Jim Nill, Assistant General Manager (Detroit Red Wings)

Gerry O'Flaherty, Pro Scout (Tampa Bay Lightning)

Larry Pleau, Former NHL General Manager (St. Louis Blues)

Kevin Prendergast, Head Scout (Hockey Canada)

Terry Richardson, Amateur Scout (Washington Capitals)

Doug Rose, Hockey Skills Coach

Greg Royce, Amateur Scout (Ottawa Senators)

Mark Seidel, Director of Scouting (NACS)

Harkie Singh, Former NHL Scout

Marty Stein, Amateur Scout (Detroit Red Wings)

Geoff Stevens, Amateur Scout (New Jersey Devils)

Trevor Timmins, Director of Player Recruitment (Montreal Canadiens)

Brad Treliving, Assistant General Manager (Phoenix Coyotes)

John Williams, Assistant Director of Amateur Scouting (Columbus Blue Jackets)

Doug Wilson, General Manager (San Jose Sharks)

Jim Yaworski, Owner of Belfast Giants and Former NHL Scout

PART 1

Life at the Corner of the Rink

CHAPTER 1

An Introduction to Scouting

"It's easy to go out to a game and pick out the best players. Every fan knows the guy who got the hat trick that night probably is one of the better players in the game. But it's not easy to go to the game and see the guy on the fourth line who had five shifts, did everything right, played his position, had good read and react, and is a big skinny guy who, once he gets strength, is going to be an above average skater and contribute down the road. It takes time and patience and a lot of practice to fine-tune that art."

Scott Luce, Director of Amateur Scouting, Florida Panthers

Did you ever wonder how NHL teams decide which teenagers have the stuff to live out their dreams and become NHL players? Well, it's the scouts who make that possible—working tirelessly behind the scenes and examining thousands of prospective players in order to select the one or two who will become a perfect addition to their team. *The Art of Scouting* is for any hockey fan who has ever been curious about what really happens in the secret world of scouting hockey. Its storytelling is combined with insights from some of the best scouts in the business, including the scouts' views on particular aspects of the art of scouting and their individual opinions and tales of observation.

Scouting is an industry with a rich history and unique culture. *The Art of Scouting* gives readers an inside look at how the scouting world of today came to be and at its foundation, which is the hard work and camaraderie of the scouts. It also examines how prospects are evaluated and developed. During a prospect's pivotal draft year, scouts must determine if he has what it takes to become an elite-level player, and I share with you the in-depth analysis that scouts use to make these assessments. Through my discussions with scouts, directors of amateur scouting, directors of player personnel, and assistant general managers, I bring to light the secretive trade of deciding who plays in the NHL and who does not.

There is no more difficult job in the entire game of hockey than that of an amateur scout, and the game would suffer if not for the dedication of these individuals. Players face an arduous journey to the NHL; there are injuries, pitfalls, and roadblocks challenging these young prospects, and scouts have to analyze all of this in order to make the best selections for their teams. Despite the impact scouting has on the success of a team, little is known about it because there has never been a book that delved deeply into how scouts scout—until now.

THE EVOLUTION OF SCOUTING

The scouting traditions and the mindset of the industry all stem from the original scouts who forged the trail. Like everything else, scouting has evolved over the years. It has changed from a small group of bird dogs in the days of the Original Six to the current environment, which includes 30 NHL scouting departments and an NHL Central Scouting bureau.

Tim Burke, Director of Scouting, San Jose Sharks, remembers how small the scouting fraternity was back in his early days. The number of scouts and the vast areas they must scour for talent have increased dramatically in the last 20 years. Anytime a group expands its numbers, some of the relationships inevitably change. While the new generation of scouts adds to the tapestry, the sheer numbers result in a less tightly knit community.

> *"Back in the late '80s we were at a Four Nations Tournament. There were 15 scouts at the Four Nations. Jack Button took a picture and mailed it to me a month later. Fifteen scouts! So in '87, '88, every year you had the same group of guys going over there, and now you go to one of those tournaments and there are over 200 scouts, it's unbelievable. We used to travel in Europe like a travelling road show, with characters like J.C. Tremblay and Gerry Melynk. Every one of them loved their team when you go back and think about it, and they respected other scouts. It wasn't like now; there are so many of them that it's hard to really get to know the people as well."*

Not only has the size of the industry grown, but so have the technological advancements. Although observing the game live is still the primary tool for scouts, how they collect and manage the information they obtain has certainly changed. Lou Jankowski was a scout for the New York Rangers in the early days, and his son, second-generation NHL scout Ryan Jankowski, recalls his father's challenges.

> *"I would come home from school a lot of days and he'd be sitting at the kitchen table writing out his reports. Hand writing his reports, hand writing his expenses—that's what they did back then. There were no computers, there were no fancy gadgets that there are now, like the BlackBerrys and Palm Pilots, where you can do them right at the rink. I'd say that was the essence of scouting; that's when it was in its purest form. We tend to overcomplicate things now because of the technology that we have. Whereas back then, there were three reports, you know, that the scouts would do. They would do like a November report, they'd do a mid-season report, and they'd do a year-end report on these players. It'd be a triplicate copy, there would be a white copy, a pink copy, and a yellow copy. Well, the white and pink ones would go to New York and the yellow one would stay in his filing cabinet downstairs."*

Ryan Jankowski, Amateur Scout, Montreal Canadiens

THE LIFE OF AN AMATEUR SCOUT

When you see a group of men huddled over their coffees in the corner of the rink, odds are they're hockey scouts. They like to watch their prospective players from the corner of the rink because it provides an unobstructed view of all aspects of a player's game—the good, the bad, and the ugly.

Recruiting the right players is so critical to the success of NHL teams that they dedicate entire departments to the pursuit. But what exactly do scouts do, besides spend a lot of time freezing their butts off at the rink and drinking bad coffee? Essentially, they scour arenas all over the globe in search of players who can, eventually, help their team win a Stanley Cup.

Generally, if amateur scouts are working from their home base, they will devote time in the morning to watching game film from the previous night's games. They will be looking for any clues they may have missed while watching the games live. If the schedule works out, the scouts will also watch the morning practices of the local junior teams and perhaps speak to the coaches and players. Most scouts have two or three junior or college teams in their area, which means they can watch a game six days a week (on average) without travelling. On a game night, the scouts congregate in a designated room at the arena about an hour and a half before the game to prepare and talk shop with their brethren. Each scout has a booklet where he notes the team's lineups and scratches and where he designates which players he will focus on that night. After the game is over, scouts head down to the dressing rooms to speak to players or coaches and collect additional information for their reports. Then they drive home, finish their scouting reports, and type them into the database while everything is still fresh in their minds.

Their routine changes slightly when they must travel to see prospects in another part of the region or in another part of the country. Depending on the location, a scout may drive five or six hours, check into a hotel, find a restaurant so he can get something to eat, and then shuffle off to the rink. Now, it may seem like fun being out on the hunt for the next NHL star and, for the most part, it is. However, imagine being away from your family for 10 days or more every month and travelling the icy back roads in Saskatchewan. It's all the little things that wear on scouts, like having to deal with airports, rental cars, changing hotels, and finding a decent meal. Anyone who has travelled for work understands that this lifestyle can drain the body and mind, especially considering most of the locales scouts visit are not exotic. And this ritual goes on from September to May every year—no wonder scouts all look haggard by the end of the season.

Throughout the hockey season, NHL scouting departments have meetings with all of their amateur scouts to discuss the players they have seen. This allows them to get information on the players who will make up their final list heading into the NHL Entry Draft. Each organization has certain characteristics that they favour in a player, and this allows the scouts to narrow their search. Once prospects have been physically and psychologically evaluated at the NHL combine, scouts have one final meeting to compile their list of preferred players for the Draft. In addition, most NHL scouting departments will gather a few days before the Draft to hash over any last-minute strategies and information. This also gives teams one last chance to meet with players directly and get a final impression of the young men they might select.

"There are two factions of the hockey world that are completely overlooked. One is the trainers and the

equipment managers and the second is the amateur scouts. The lifeblood of any organization is the talent that the amateur scouts find year in and year out, and these guys only have two days to do their job. They do their job the whole year, but they only have two days where it is showtime. That is extremely difficult, but the best ones seemingly do it right all the time."

Pierre McGuire, TSN Broadcaster

SUCCESSFUL SCOUTS

So, what makes a successful scout? Is it as easy as choosing the best player on each respective junior or college team? Or is there an art and learned skill to finding a diamond in the rough? Scouting would certainly be easier if there was a guidebook handed down from one scout to another, but to my knowledge no such magic tome exists. Scouting is a combination of gathering hard facts and relying on gut feelings. Scouts have to be one part detective, one part art appraiser, and one part psychologist (and owning a crystal ball doesn't hurt either). While there is no blueprint for becoming a successful scout, having an open mind, patience, plus good research and interpersonal skills are all critical. Good scouts are able to self-analyze and look back over previous choices so they can analyze what did and did not work in order to avoid repeating mistakes.

What qualifies as success for a scout? At the end of their season, after thousands of games, videos, and interviews, how does a team measure a scout's success? According to a variety of NHL general managers and directors of amateur scouting, the consensus is that the goal is to get two NHL players out of every Draft. Since each Draft now consists of seven rounds, that means only two of the seven or more players selected by a team each year will successfully reach the NHL.

> *"It's the only job where you can be right 15 percent of the time and be ruled a Hall of Famer or a success. You are going to be wrong 85 or 80 percent of the time, and if you hit on 2.5 home runs every Draft, you are par with some of the best scouts ever."*
>
> Mike Futa, Co-Director of Amateur Scouting,
> Los Angeles Kings

THE NHL ENTRY DRAFT

In June of each year, all the NHL teams gather for the NHL Entry Draft. Created in 1963, the Draft provides teams with the opportunity to select players who are entering the NHL for the first time. Eligible players include North Americans and Europeans who are 17–20 years old.

All of the work scouts do throughout the year culminates at the NHL Entry Draft. That's right, all those months of work and countless hours of watching hockey come down to two days in June, when all the information they have gathered is condensed into the list of players that their teams would like to acquire. The NHL holds a lottery to decide the order in which the teams get to make the first 14 picks. After that, the order is based on how the teams performed during the previous season. The lottery system helps to limit the risk of teams "throwing games" in order to earn a better draft pick.

Scouts find the Draft both exciting and nerve-racking. After all of their hard work and research, they must come together with their team and reach a consensus about which players will be the best fit for their organization. Then they must cross their fingers and hope that a team with a higher pick than them doesn't want the same player. Even if they manage to land the player of their dreams, they still have to wait for him to develop before they find out if they've made the right decision, and that development can take up to five years or more. And yet apparently the whole exercise is fun for scouts, because as soon as the Draft ends, they begin the process all over again.

CHAPTER 2

Amateur and Professional Scouting

"They both have their tough part with different variables, but on the amateur side, the projection makes it very challenging and on the Pro side, you are getting more of the finished product, but you are still looking for that diamond in the rough."

Jim Nill, Assistant General Manager, Detroit Red Wings

To help them find players, teams employ two types of scouts: amateur and professional. On the surface they may seem like the same job, but they are actually quite different. Each has its own function within the hockey operations department and the decisions made by these scouts can alter the course of an NHL organization dramatically. The majority of the decisions at the NHL Draft and the decisions about whether to trade for or sign a player from the non-professional ranks come from the amateur scouting department. Their primary focus is to assist the NHL organization in collecting assets for the long-term future. The scouts on the professional side make recommendations on players who can be acquired via the free agency or trade routes. Pro scouts focus on whether a player can fit directly into the system the team is already playing, and their player selections fulfill a more immediate need than those of the amateur scouts.

After much first-hand observation and many discussions with scouts about the distinct differences between the two types of scouting, I believe amateur scouting is the more challenging discipline to learn. *Bruce Haralson*, Pro Scout, Detroit Red Wings, notes one of the main differences between the two types of scouting:

> *"The biggest difference between amateur and pro scouting is that in amateur you are dealing with kids aged 16 to 20 as opposed to watching the pro ranks, who would be primarily age 20 and up."*

AMATEUR SCOUTS

Amateur scouts are employed by their NHL team to search primarily all of the non-professional leagues for players who might be valuable additions to the team, either through the NHL Draft or through unrestricted free agency. Both junior and college teams also have scouts who watch the minor leagues for players, but they are not the focus of this book.

Amateur scouts:

- assess college and junior league players,
- put together a list of players who interest them,

- fully evaluate the players on that list,
- try to project the abilities of the players out into the future to determine whether or not they'll be able to compete at the next level, and finally,
- rank the players based on all of this information.

On page 16 there is a sample organizational chart to help you understand who plays what role in choosing the amateur talent for an NHL team.

While each team gives its scouts a different mandate for the type of players they're looking for, scouts generally look at the following areas of a player's game: hockey sense, other intangibles (such as leadership ability), skating, puck skills, shooting, physical game, and positional play (forward, defence, or goalie). Each of these areas is discussed in depth later in this book.

Scouts spend the entire year examining and evaluating players, and the teams use their final rankings to make their player selections at the annual NHL Draft. And following those two days in June, they start the process all over again with a new crop of junior-aged players.

Bruce Haralson notes that the set of variables for an amateur scout is mind-boggling.

"When you are evaluating amateurs for the potential to become an NHL player, you are looking at many different variables—skill, hockey sense, skating ability, and size, so all that weighs into scouting amateurs."

The projection of the young prospects is one of the biggest challenges according to *Haralson*. Amateur scouts must not

---

Director of Amateur Scouting

Responsible for coordinating the duties of the amateur scouts and for setting the mandate for what type of players the GM is seeking for the NHL Draft. Also manages the scouting reports on the team database and runs the amateur scouting meetings.

↓

Assistant Director of Amateur Scouting

Assists the director of amateur scouting with all of his duties. (Usually only teams with a large scouting staff employ one.)

↓

Regional Scouts (full- and part-time)

Each scout is responsible for evaluating prospects in a certain region, such as Western Canada and the United States, Ontario, Sweden, Czech Republic, and so on.

---

only determine the physical attributes of a player, but also the mental capabilities. Without the benefit of a crystal ball, they have to give it their best educated guess about whether and when the player's abilities will all come together.

"The big thing is to project these youngsters and what they are capable of when they reach their early twenties. So, not only are you trying to project their physical abilities

but also their mental abilities, and it takes a lot of mental toughness to play the pro game. As an amateur scout you are trying to look into their future at what they can become, as opposed to pro scouting where you are evaluating players already in the AHL or NHL."

Tod Button, Director of Scouting, Calgary Flames, scouts both amateurs and professionals throughout the year, and bouncing between the two thought processes is no easy feat. The burning question in his mind when watching an amateur prospect is: "How much better will he become?" He needs to decide—if the prospect gets assistance from the team through his prime development years, will that be enough for him to become an NHL player?

"When you're scouting amateur when the kids are first-year NHL Draft eligible and they are 17 years old, not only are you trying to figure out where they are physically and mentally, but you also have to determine how their skill set can change or improve. How much better do they have to get at those skills and can physical development help that?"

Jim Nill, Assistant General Manager, Detroit Red Wings, agrees that predicting how a player will develop, and if he will at all, is one of the toughest parts of amateur scouting. The varying development cycles of prospects, not only physically but mentally and emotionally, too, all make amateur scouting a head spinner. Even with all the background work and research they do on a prospect, *Nill* thinks that amateur scouts are still left with many unanswered questions.

> *"The toughest part of amateur scouting is the projection part. You're looking at kids that are 16, 17, and 18 years of age and trying to see what they are at 24 or 25. Some kids at 17 have already peaked physically; they are mature at 6-foot-2 and 200 pounds and they may not change anymore. Then there are other players that are 5-foot-10 and 170 pounds, and they are going to hit a growth spurt and end up 6-foot-3 and 220. Those late bloomers may overtake the ones that were mature at a younger age."*

Another factor that *Nill* brings up is the various playing situations that the prospects are put into while playing in the juniors. For example, the number of games played over a short period of time can have a marked impact on the quality of a prospect's game. Scouts must be careful to take these variables into consideration when making their determinations and projections.

> *"The other thing is the age you are dealing with and projection, especially when you go to the junior game and the kid rode the bus eight hours then played the game. That's hard to do, and these kids might be playing four games in six nights and busing eight hours every night to get to the next game. You might catch him on the last game of that road trip and they have nothing left, and a scout has to sit there and try to judge him."*

Having scouted both amateurs and professionals, *Nill* admits the amateur scouting department has the harder task.

He makes reference to the collective bargaining agreement (CBA) as an obstacle. The pressure on the amateur scouts and the player development departments to produce players is at an all-time high. With the new salary constraints, the pro scouts have limited opportunity to bail out the amateur side if a player doesn't develop as expected.

> *"The amateur side is so tough because of the projection. Also, the amateur side has become a big part of this new CBA, so you must have young kids coming up through the system. Once an organization has signed their core six players to long-term contracts, there is no more movement for making trades to really get better. So you are depending on the amateur side to find some players that can come up and make an impact. You're hoping it'll happen in a short period of time because you need young players that are making a lower-level salary and can make an impact on your team."*

Tom Kurvers, Assistant General Manager, Tampa Bay Lightning, admires the amateur scouts who go out year after year and dig for the one or two diamonds who will make a difference for their team.

> *"I have an easier time of it because I've spent much more time on the pro side. The amateur scouts are after the 'can't miss players' who still have a chance to miss. It's a lot more projection, a lot more homework trying to sort out their character when you don't have solid information from the outset. You know, the best scouts are the ones that dig the hardest, and that's a lot of work with people. Then it*

turns over every calendar year, because immediately after the Draft you are on to the next batch of players.''

It's often the off-ice variables that can make or break a player's career according to *Kurvers*. How he navigates those waters is crucial, as is the judgement the scout has to make about whether or not he can do it successfully.

"I think amateur scouting is more difficult. You are talking about way more variables—young men who are maturing and they are showing what they need to show to give you an idea that they can get better. But there are still hurdles they've got to jump, and they have to get bigger, stronger, faster. They have to make all the adjustments of living, maybe going to college, maybe going from junior hockey into the American league and then to the NHL.''

PROFESSIONAL SCOUTS

The general consensus is that pro scouts have a slightly easier time than amateur scouts do. Pro scouts watch the professional leagues, including the NHL, AHL, ECHL, and the European leagues. As *Tom Kurvers* points out, all the players coming through those pro ranks to the NHL were once considered good by a scout.

"Someone at some point has made an educated bet that this player is worth signing to a contract. They are going to get a chance as a pro, so they have been scouted and they have been deemed worthy of a chance. So you take that into consideration the first time you see a guy who has played pro.''

Professional scouts are employed by their NHL team to search all of the professional leagues for players who might be valuable additions to the team, either through trades, waiver additions, or free agency.

Professional scouts:

- assess professional players from leagues such as the NHL, AHL, ECHL, and Europe,
- put together a list of players who interest them,
- fully evaluate the players on that list,
- try to project the abilities of the players to determine whether they'll be able to fit within the organization's style of play, and finally,
- rank the players based on all of this information.

On the following page is a sample organizational chart to help you understand who plays what role in choosing the professional talent for an NHL team.

The evaluation process for a pro scout is somewhat different than for an amateur scout. Pro scouts must have their team's philosophy in mind and look for players who would fit in easily with an already established team. By the time they've reached the pro ranks, players have demonstrated that they have a certain level of skills. Usually pro scouts are looking for specific skills and attributes that will fill a current need on their team (i.e., a right-shooting defensive centre). *Bruce Haralson* points out that pro scouting does still involve some projection, primarily because the players are drafted at such a young age to begin with.

Director of Professional Scouting

Responsible for coordinating the duties of the professional scouts and for setting the mandate for what type of players the GM is seeking for immediate roster upgrades. Also manages the scouting reports on the team database and runs the pro scouting meetings.

↓

Assistant Director of Professional Scouting

Assists the director of professional scouting with all of his duties. (Usually only teams with a large scouting staff employ one.)

↓

European Professional Head Scout

Responsible for coordinating the duties of the professional scouts in Europe and for setting the mandate for what type of players the GM is seeking for the immediate roster upgrades. Manages the European scouting reports on the team database. (Again, not every team will employ one of these.)

↓

Regional Scouts (full- and part-time)

Each scout is responsible for a certain region, such as the Western Conference NHL and AHL, the Eastern Conference NHL and AHL, and the professional European leagues.

"In pro scouting you're looking at players in the professional leagues across the world. Now, if they are young guys, obviously they are still developing, so you are trying to

determine how good they can be at the NHL level. In some cases it can take two, three, four, or five years for players to develop to that stage."

Tod Button makes it clear that not all pro leagues are the same. From his point of view, a great deal depends on what age group and development cycle the players are in. He feels that during the first few years of a player's pro career he must be scouted differently than both amateur players and more established pros. At that age and development level, they straddle the line between amateur and pro scouting.

"There are different levels of pro hockey, and specifically when you are watching the pros in their entry level. That's the biggest difference. Once a player is 21 or 22 and in the middle of their entry-level contract, you are trying to determine what they are going to be at the NHL level. Are they going to be a skilled forward or a two-way guy? How are they going to contribute to your team and how much more development do they need?"

Once players reach the age of 24 and beyond, *Button* says they are scouted differently. At this stage, the pro scouts are not projecting a developing player but rather are trying to see if he fits a role within their system. Finding players who can fit a role is not as easy as it sounds, since players thrive under different circumstances.

"Once they are 24 to 25, it's way more of how they fit on your team and how they can help your team in a specific role. Is he going to be a top-line centre or a left wing on the second line? Is he a power player that is more defined

because they already have the physical tools? You know as a scout whether they are a good skater or they are strong enough, now it's more a question of can they fit into your team instead of can they even make it to the NHL."

Because *Bruce Haralson* scouts for Detroit and they primarily play a puck-possession style, those types of players are his priority.

"In terms of evaluating them at a pro level, you are looking for free agency, future trades, and how they would fit into your system. A lot of teams play different styles, and the Red Wings have been a puck-possession team for a while. In turn, I'm scouting other players to see if they can fit into our system and to evaluate their ability to adapt and hang on to the puck. So in terms of skills, we are looking for guys with the higher skill level."

The philosophy of an NHL team and the style of game it plays can make finding the right player seem like searching for a needle in a haystack. The world of pro scouts is less cookie cutter than amateur scouting, where the prospects they draft have years to develop. The pro scouts are given specific types of players to target for their organization, and that can change from year to year or even month to month. The need to find players is always immediate for pro scouts. *Bruce Haralson* says it's challenging to find a player who fits into their system and who has been overlooked by other teams. It's the balance of being able to play a puck-possession style and still have an element of toughness that is the key for him.

"There are big physical players that play this game, and they are primarily here for one reason—to provide a physical presence a team covets. In our case, and I can only go off what we do in the Red Wings, and it's not that we don't like guys that are physical and compete, it's just not as important for us. We would much prefer a guy who can think and who has the skill to play the game at a high level. But by the same token, if they can compete on an everyday basis in all situations, that's good. Now, they do not have to go out there and beat the hell out of people, but at the same time, they have to be able to take the hits to make the plays. That's something in our organization that has become very important over the years."

When the new collective bargaining agreement was reached, pro scouting became more challenging than ever, according to *Jim Nill*. In the past, a team could sign the best player available for their system, but now the restrictive salary structure can blow up a plan instantly.

"On the pro side you are getting more of the finished product, but you are still looking for that diamond in the rough. You kind of know the players, but you are looking for that one guy that is going to fit into the puzzle for your team. The dynamics of the CBA has changed so much now that the salary becomes a factor even at the AHL and in Europe. Before, a scout was just comparing player for player, but now a lot of it depends on the contract and does it fit into your team structure. You might love a player, but at $4 million you can't love him anymore, and that's the toughest part of pro scouting now."

Pro scouting is a much more long-term process than amateur scouting. While the amateur scouts start fresh again each year after the Draft, the pros can spend a decade watching the same players. Patience and perseverance are key attributes for a successful pro scout.

> *"In amateur it's always new, whereas in pro scouting you start picking up on players at maybe age 19 or 20 at the earliest. A scout might be scouting that player over the course of 10 or 12 years and watching his evolution progress. You know, there might be a point in time where you like the player, don't like the player, like him again."*
>
> Tom Kurvers

At the end of the day, *John Ferguson Jr.* believes remembering that this is a business and that the players are assets is the key to creating a successful NHL team. He thinks the amateur and pro scouts must work in unison and understand the value of every player on the market as it pertains to their particular organization. As long as the scouts on both sides are fully invested in the philosophy of the player development department and keep an open mind, they'll do well.

> *"You are managing assets and must learn to continue to grow the asset value, especially if you've got expiring contracts in players who might be moving on. What I mean is, it's important to make sure that you are assessing those prospects and then turning them into additional assets. Focus on what you need and put it into context not just for this week or this month, but looking forward to the following season and even years out."*

CHAPTER 3

Where to Find Them

"We are taking all these players from all different ways of playing the game and different cultures, and we're trying to put them into a small league of 30 teams."
Gordie Clark, Director of Player Personnel, New York Rangers

NHL Draft history has shown that success in the NHL can't be based on junior-league achievement alone. After all, how many times have fans seen a top NHL draft pick not make it to the big league while a fifth-round choice goes on to a successful NHL career? Why does this happen? Well, consider that potential draft picks are scouted the world over—from Vernon, British Columbia, to Moscow, Russia, and all points in between. The vast mileage that scouts record in any given year during their search for the next great player would make even a travel agent's head spin.

Given all the different leagues that scouts must view, making an accurate comparison between prospects becomes almost impossible. This issue is compounded because scouts must not only compare the prospects with each other but also against current NHL players. They must try to project whether or not the teenage prospects will develop into players who can compete in the NHL. Clearly, scouting different levels of players from different calibre leagues and then predicting their future abilities will never be an exact science. *Craig Button*, Former NHL General Manager, agrees:

"There is no exact science in that and there never will be, and anyone that suggests there is, is completely wrong. That's why projection is such a key part in scouting—you don't get the opportunity to say, 'Let's take Sidney Crosby at 17 and test him against Nick Lidstrom,' so for the most part, you as a scout have to evaluate those players against players that are not anywhere near that level of competition."

To keep his staff organized, *Gordie Clark*, Director of Player Personnel, New York Rangers, started to put prospects into categories. While doing this, he sat down with his staff and mulled over how many teams he and his scouts see in any given season.

"We tried to count how many junior teams we have to cover in the world—WHL, OHL, QMJHL, USHL, NAHL, Tier-II all across Canada, New England has three or four different leagues, prep schools, high schools, NCAA, and

the Swedes, Finns, Czechs, Slovaks, and Russians all have leagues—and it was over 300 teams."

THE LEAGUES

Since most hockey fans don't have the luxury of seeing all the prospects up close and in person, understanding their favourite team's draft choices can be difficult. They need to remember that there are nine areas where the vast majority of NHL prospects are uncovered by scouts, and inside those areas there are over 300 teams to choose from. These figures are daunting for NHL scouting departments—how can they figure out which prospects to watch within the limited amount of time they have?

To give you some insight into the choices teams have, I offer a brief explanation of the leagues and regions and how the scouts perceive the different leagues. How a prospect has been coached, developed on and off the ice, and the impact of that culture directly affect when and where a player is drafted.

Junior Hockey in Canada

Traditionally, junior hockey in Canada has been the largest provider of talent to the NHL for generations. Due to the similar style of play and the number of games they play, coupled with the extensive travel, junior hockey in Canada is the closest mirror to the NHL. What cannot be understated is the strong bond junior hockey teams have with their respective communities. That bond unites the entire hockey team and the community with passion and fanaticism. There are two main junior leagues in Canada that provide talent to the

NHL: the Canadian Hockey League and the Canadian Junior A Hockey League.

Canadian Hockey League (CHL)

The majority of NHL players come out of the Canadian Hockey League, which consists of three leagues: the 18-team Quebec Junior Hockey League, the 20-team Ontario Hockey League, and the 22-team Western Hockey League. The league includes teams from across Canada and from nine U. S. cities.

The Memorial Cup is the CHL's version of the Stanley Cup, and it has almost as much tradition. Every spring, the top teams from the QMJHL, OHL, and WHL duke it out for major-junior hockey supremacy. The CHL is similar in structure to the professional leagues and is considered a faster track to the NHL.

"There is a world of difference between the leagues. The Canadian Hockey League is the closest to pro, so you are watching a player in an environment that is closest to the pro's."

Rick Dudley, General Manager, Atlanta Thrashers

While it's the league where most successful NHL prospects are developed, *Tim Burke* notes that obstacles in the evaluation process still crop up—like the CHL's tough schedule. When a young prospect plays multiple games in a short period of time, the effects cannot be overlooked.

"For example, Niagara is playing their third game in a row in Saginaw on a Sunday, and I am looking at two or three

guys on that team. I have to give the guys the benefit of the
doubt. Maybe their energy isn't what I want it to be, but I
have to look beyond that."

Canadian Junior A Hockey League (CJHL)

The Canadian Junior A League is considered a less competitive
and less skilled league than the Canadian Hockey League. The
CJHL has 10 leagues and 137 teams across Canada and, despite
not attracting much national media attention, it's the largest
league in the world. It's structured differently than the CHL,
and one of the most noticeable differences is that players in
the CJHL are not given a stipend, which means they retain
their eligibility to earn NCAA scholarships.

At the end of each season, the top four CJHL teams battle
it out at the national championship for the prestigious Royal
Bank Cup (previously called the Centennial Cup). Some of the
NHL's biggest stars began their career in this league, including
Steve Yzerman, Curtis Joseph, Brett Hull, Paul Kariya, and
Dany Heatley.

"We have the Tier-II junior leagues, which is a step below
major junior, but it is a pretty good league in itself. You
have to try and watch a player in that league and compare
him against players you know can play at the major-junior
level."

Rick Dudley

Junior Hockey in the United States

Over the past two decades, the U.S. junior hockey leagues
have made tremendous progress in developing players who

consistently make the NHL. Now, there are multiple junior leagues in the United States, but three are the focus of most NHL scouts: the United States Hockey League (USHL), the North American Hockey League (NAHL), and the Eastern Junior Hockey League (EJHL), each of which brings a unique flavour and varying skill level. Both the USHL and NAHL have worked directly with and played games against the United States National Development Program.

Jim Hammett, NHL Scout, thinks the talent level has improved in all three of these leagues. However, projections about players' abilities are still a little less certain than those of their counterparts in the CHL. Although scouts may have to spend a little more time projecting and doing background work in the U. S. leagues, *Hammett* thinks it can be well worth it in the end.

> *"It takes a little bit more projection, and when you are talking about those leagues you are talking about guys that are going to be, for the most part, trying to pursue a college scholarship. So sometimes they are four or five years away from being a pro, but they are all quality leagues and they can't be ignored. That's where the importance of your area scouts comes into play. They have to know those leagues like the back of their hands and really have to do a good job on their background, and if they do that, they are still going to find a really good player in those leagues."*

United States Hockey League (USHL)

This league attracts players from all over the globe and has made excellent strides, recently being granted Tier-I status—making it the only Tier-I junior league in the country. The USHL has 15 member teams and limits enrolment to players who are 20 years of age or younger. Their final championship, the Clark Cup, is always exciting, and this league is an excellent base from which junior hockey will grow in the United States. The ongoing relationship with USA Hockey has helped this league develop into the premier junior hockey league in the United States.

North American Hockey League (NAHL)

Founded in 1975, the NAHL is the oldest Junior A hockey league in the United States. The Tier-II league has grown to 26 member teams spread over four divisions and currently includes teams from as far north as Alaska and as far south as Texas.

Eastern Junior Hockey League (EJHL)

The EJHL was founded in 1993. This Tier-III league includes 14 teams from across the northeastern United States.

> *"I think the USHL, NAHL, EJHL are really starting to produce a lot of hockey players, as is anywhere in the USA. Before, we had sort of the traditional areas like Minnesota, Wisconsin, Michigan, Illinois, and parts of New England, but now we are seeing players come out of Florida, Texas, and California. I think it helped that the NHL progressed and started to get teams in different markets. It takes a while for the minor hockey to develop, but eventually they start to produce."*
>
> Ross Mahoney, Director of Amateur Scouting,
> Washington Capitals

USA National Training Development Program

Created by USA Hockey in 1996, the National Training Development Program trains players under the age of 20 to compete on the U.S. national teams. In addition to representing the United States at select international tournaments, its two teams also compete regularly at home, participating against a variety of opponents such as NAHL, USHL, and NCAA teams.

> *"I think the U.S. national program is probably getting 75 to 80 percent of the top U.S. kids each year for the NHL draft. The benefit to scouting that program is there are kids that play on that team who are first round to seventh round picks. If you see someone playing against that team, it's very comparable. In other words, you watch that team play in the USHL and you get a good read on USHL players. Some of those kids will play in international tournaments against some of the better Canadian teams, but you never know based on what type of team they are able to put together which players are available at that time and how they go head-to-head against the Europeans."*
>
> Mark Kelley, Director of Amateur Scouting,
> Chicago Blackhawks

National College Athletic Association (NCAA)

The U.S. college players play fewer games than their junior league counterparts, and the league provides a slower maturation process for them. The five-conference, 57-team association boasts the best college hockey players on the planet. Many U.S. Junior, Canadian Junior A League, and European players become student athletes in the NCAA, which draws audiences from across North America and Europe. And the entire continent comes together to watch the annual National Championship, known as The Frozen Four.

"College is an up-tempo game with a lot of contact in it, but for the most part they are smaller players compared to major junior."

Rick Dudley

U.S. High Schools and Prep Schools

Perhaps the most challenging places to scout potential NHLers are the high school and prep school hockey leagues, due to the lack of talent. The length of their schedules, locations, and lack of competition are all factors that contribute to the difficulty in projecting these players accurately, according to *Rick Dudley*.

"When you are talking about drafting a high school player, you are watching a player that plays at a level that is considerably below the NCAA, junior, or European leagues, and that makes it a difficult process."

Dudley points out these difficulties are not limited to hockey. Other sports also have a hard time projecting accurately at the high school level, even baseball, which has the benefit of practical statistical analysis.

"You go back to baseball and there is the book Money Ball that discusses not drafting high school players because the level of play is so much different. A 0.435 hitter in high school doesn't translate the same into college or triple A

ball or MLB, and in hockey you have a little bit of the same thing."

The high school and prep school teams are spread out across the country. The variety of talent, number of games played, and coaching all impact the quality of prospects and their development. The scouts also have to take into account the level of competition in each region, as some teams only play within their respective states. We have all seen a high school kid make the transition to the NHL quickly, but they are a rarity. But it's those diamonds in the rough that keep scouts coming back to scour the high school teams.

"When you look at the high school situation, it can be interesting. A lot of times that player you are watching is the oldest player on his team, compared to if you are watching a 17- or 18-year-old player from major junior or college where they are probably on the younger range on their team, so there are different challenges for sure."

Ross Mahoney

European Leagues

The mass influx of European-born stars to the NHL since the late '80s and the impact they have had on the game of hockey confirm that the European leagues are fertile territory for scouts. However, the many differences between the North American game and the European one are an issue. In addition, the individual countries each have their own unique aspects, which makes projecting these prospects even more complex. The atmospheric and cultural differences between the countries make for a myriad of development styles and attitudes that scouts must dissect.

"You go to Europe and you watch an entirely different approach to the game. It's not nearly as physical, and it's much more skilled. Then you have to determine whether a very young player can translate his game to the NHL."

Rick Dudley

"If you go to a junior game in Sweden, there is nobody in the stands and there is no band and no real hype or excitement, and you say to yourself, 'just watch the little things that are happening.'"

Tim Burke

The Big Five: Russia, Czech Republic, Slovakia, Finland, Sweden

The five most predominant European hockey nations all have produced Hockey Hall of Fame–calibre players. Each country continues to make its mark on the NHL by developing prospects. However, as fans may have noticed, the quality and quantity of players from each nation can vary depending on the development cycle. Which nation produces the best prospects for the NHL is a debate that may never be settled. But the cultures of certain countries make the transition easier for prospects who leave their homes for North America.

"When you are looking to draft a player out of the European leagues, the most important thing to have is a strong regional scout in that area who has a good track record of understanding how each particular prospect has been developed and how the country they are from develops players. When you are looking at drafting players from Sweden and Finland, they are fairly North American in

terms of using up-to-date training techniques and so that transition can be pretty straightforward."

Scott Luce, Director of Amateur Scouting,

Florida Panthers

The Developing Hockey Nations: Germany, Switzerland, Latvia, Slovenia, Belarus, Kazakhstan, Norway

These seven developing hockey nations all have minor hockey associations that are at various stages of producing NHL talent. The number of quality players from these countries has risen dramatically over the last 20 years, and that is a promising sign. It's important for scouts not to overlook these nations as their programs develop further, especially since the need for quality NHL prospects has never been more desperate.

"There are players there, so we have to go to those countries and cover those tournaments and step up and take a player from that region if we believe in him. Now, there are more players in recent years coming out of Denmark, Switzerland, and Germany, and the hockey is really improving in those countries. You can't lose sight of those players even though those countries have not produced many players in the past."

Ross Mahoney

WORLD JUNIOR TOURNAMENTS

In addition to watching the leagues mentioned above, scouts also converge on the annual Under-18, and -20 World Junior Championships in their search for NHL-calibre prospects. These are all prospect-laden tournaments and are hosted by the IIHF. They generally feature countries such as Canada,

United States, Sweden, Finland, Russia, Slovakia, Germany, Switzerland, and Belarus. Each country's National Federation will draw eligible players to represent their country from a variety of leagues from across the globe. These games provide an ideal opportunity for scouts to get a better idea of how the diverse prospects measure up against one another. Some of the greatest players in the world have participated in this tournament, including Evgeni Malkin, Victor Hedman, Zach Parise, and Ryan Getzlaf.

World Junior Championship U20

"When you are talking about the WJC tournament and a draft-eligible prospect, anybody that can step up their game and be a key component of their national team—it bodes well for them to become a quality NHL player down the road. You take a look at some of the players that have success at those tournaments, like a Marian Hossa, and there are many players that have done the same."

Trevor Timmins, Director of Player Recruitment,
Montreal Canadiens

World Junior Championship U18

"The world U18 championship is at the end of the season. A lot of those kids, especially the Europeans, have had a long season so they don't have a lot of energy left in their tanks. But at the same time, you get to see them against their peer group and see if they can step up and be leaders on their team. If they do have success, it usually gives them a boost when it comes to NHL Draft time."

Trevor Timmins

"I think it's important because they are playing on centre stage, and as a scout you get the good and the bad, but you can't make a decision on a prospect if he has one good tournament. You have to watch him all year long from his club team to the major tournaments, and that's why it is hard to send a guy to Europe one time because he has not seen them develop from the summertime on to the April tournament. You know that as a scout you can't get too high or too low on the performance at those tournaments. But they are still valuable, every time you see a player it's valuable."

Keith Gretzky, Director of Amateur Scouting,
Phoenix Coyotes

World U17 Challenge

"At the U17 WC it's an identification process, and I'm not sure if all 30 NHL teams send scouts but certainly many teams do. Perhaps not their head guys though, because there's not enough time in the hockey season to get out there and identify key prospects for the following season."

Trevor Timmins

THE CHALLENGES OF SCOUTING THE LEAGUES

The vast variety of leagues that players are drawn from makes hockey the most difficult sport to scout for. *Tim Burke* notes that it can be especially tough when the European prospects get called up and down between their elite clubs and the junior clubs. Not only does it make it more difficult to compare the calibre of player, but it also has a direct impact on the future development of the player, which a scout has to take into account as well.

> *"For example, perhaps I go to a Swedish junior game and I know Erik Karlsson has been sent down from Frolunda. He is probably figuring I am just down here for one skate and he is trying too much; I have to factor that in. And maybe a player such as Karlsson, when he is down at the junior level, is experimenting with something new and trying to do too much, and maybe he will make some mistakes. As a scout, I have to look beyond that."*

But the difficulties aren't restricted to Europe. Consider the two leagues that draw the most comparison, the CHL and the NCAA. *Tim Burke* says the different environments can cause problems for scouts.

> *"Now, you go to a college game and they are all full of piss and vinegar and the band is playing and in your mind you are thinking, 'there is a lot more going on here,' but there really is not. Then you go to a junior game where you will catch a team on a night on the road and there is no energy, and as a scout you better take all of that into consideration."*

Keeping an open mind and understanding the circumstances that the prospect is currently under is essential, especially when a scout is seeing multiple games in one day. Territorial scouts who see these kids on a regular basis are a valuable resource and make it easier to keep everything in perspective.

> *"It's no different when you're a scout in Toronto, and going to a different game each night. I have come in here on the*

*one game of this player's life right now, and then I go see
a couple of other games tonight and a couple more games
tomorrow and then in a few weeks I come back and really
want to see that player again. But in reality you have to
rely on your territory guys that sit here night after night and
see these guys way more than I do."*

Gordie Clark

For *Jim Nill*, making comparisons between players from
different leagues is the main issue. He believes that comparing
and projecting the talent of players in CHL leagues is perhaps
the easiest, while the toughest leagues to scout and project
are the high school hockey teams and the variety of European
leagues. Because the depth of talent is shallow compared to the
CHL, it's a challenge to determine if the best player in those
leagues is actually good—they don't have much competition.
The scout will have to try to compare that player's skills to
those of players in a more talented league, like the Western
Hockey League. He also warns of the need to be aware of
differing styles of play and ice surfaces, which can greatly
affect a prospect's potential in the NHL.

*"You are going to a game where maybe there is no hitting
or there is no skill other than this one player and looking at
how this player would fit into the WHL, OHL, or the college
game. That probably is the toughest part of the business,
and in Europe it's just a different style of hockey overall,
with no hitting and bigger ice."*

Gordie Clark recently drafted Chris Kreider from the high
school ranks and he says projecting was a challenge.

"I went through it with Chris Kreider who we drafted in the first round when he played high school hockey. He dominates and you can see he has top-end speed, but is he being successful because this hockey is so bad?"

"In his case, I was seeing a guy that is moving the puck and never gets it back. I was seeing a guy getting the puck in the slot and snapping it, and going down the wing and snapping these wrist shots. And you're right, that was against a prep school goalie, but if you see a guy that sees a spot and hits it, then as he goes on and develops he should project to the next level."

Craig Button points out that it's essential for scouts to make sure they understand what type of player they are evaluating. He says there is an inherent danger in envisioning a player to be something he is not. This mistake can be compounded by failing to take into account where they are playing and what type of past development they've had.

"It goes back to the scout—they better know what type of player they are looking at and evaluate him on those abilities. So if the player is a goal scorer, evaluate him on goal-scoring abilities. Whether they are in high school or major junior or over in Europe, there are certain elements of goal scoring that are true across borders and different levels. This goes the same for every position, and those are key aspects a scout has to keep in mind."

CHAPTER 4

Tools of the Trade

"The most important tools a scout has are his work ethic and what he has between his ears, and I am not saying the video and computer software is not helpful, but those two things are where it all starts."
Terry Richardson, Amateur Scout, Washington Capitals

If you speak to any scout worth their salt, they'll tell you that all the heavy lifting is done at the rink, which is where all the nuances of the game can be uncovered. There's no getting around it, scouts must spend countless hours observing their prospects at the rink. However, technological advances have changed the way scouts do business away from the rink and have become essential tools of the trade. Scouts now have access to isolated player video, customizable computer software, physical and psychological testing, and statistical analysis, all of which are valuable instruments used to help them find the next Great One.

VIDEO SCOUTING

Ever since Roger Neilson started the trend of using video as a tool to plan tactics against future opponents, video has become a valuable asset. However, scouts are quick to point out that it's not perfect and can never be considered a replacement for a real live scout. Video scouting is limited in the way it can cover the action on the ice, particularly when plays develop away from the puck.

The trend toward using more video scouting leaves a bad taste in the mouths of a few scouts, but most take it as another step in the evolution of the art of scouting. The scouts who disapprove of the trend aren't opposed to the use of video itself, but rather to scouts who use it exclusively. Just as fans who watch the game on television can miss key things that happen away from the play, so too does video. Scouts believe that nothing is more valuable than watching a live game. However, video can be very helpful. Its use varies amongst the NHL teams, with a few using it far more extensively than the others.

Scout *Mike Futa* embraces video as a tool and thinks that it will allow him and his staff to get a more accurate assessment on any player. The Los Angeles Kings have a team of video scouts who isolate game film on any player the hockey operations staff requires. In Futa's opinion, it's just common sense to use whatever tools are available to you. He points out that even though live game viewings are invaluable, scouts can still miss things while they're there.

"We have full-time video people in Los Angeles, and every game is taped. If I am interested in player X in Ontario, they will sit there in the dark and isolate that player's shifts, and

by the time I get to Los Angeles and I look in my mailbox, the tapes are there. If I have some questions whether player X protects pucks or whether his game changes if he is at home or on the road, I can check the video."

Futa has heard all about the pitfalls of video from his brethren in the scouting world, but he believes that having a Plan B or Plan C is beneficial. He points out that it's possible for scouts to miss things because of the layout of the arena or where the scout was sitting or human error. He knows that you can see a certain player multiple times and in different scenarios and still not see everything necessary to make the right decision. Video affords scouts more opportunities to examine the finer points of a prospect's game.

"Certain teams like to say, 'Well, you are cancelling out the value of live viewings,' but we have all the live viewings, just as everyone else does. With video as a backup plan, we can sit there and debate whether player X has grit or pulls up at the corners and then watch it. We isolate games and ask the coach, 'If you were going to sell us, which two kids and what were the best games they played?' Then we will get those isolated, and we can rate him against his best games and his average games and find where his consistency is."

Video simply provides additional information to the mix that must be gathered before a player is drafted, traded, or signed. *Futa* thinks accumulating as much data as possible helps to prevent (or limit) bad decisions.

"When you add up the live viewings, family and player interviews, coach interviews, practice habits, and intangibles, and then you back it up with some isolation video, you've got a better chance of being right."

Keith Gretzky also uses video scouting to supplement the information he and his team are able to gather. As he points out, he can't be at every game, so he has a staff to cut game footage on players they're interested in, and they use what they see to enhance their scouting reports.

"Anytime you have any information on a player it's useful. Video allows you to see different things and analyze different things because you can't go to every game. It's useful for our staff that doesn't get out to see those players as often. We've got guys cutting tape left and right, and if you want to key on a player, you can get a lot of footage on him."

Now, *Brent Flahr*, Assistant General Manager, Minnesota Wild, agrees with Gretzky that it's a nice supplement, but warns that nothing replaces watching the live game. *Flahr* thinks video misses the little nuances of the game, especially away from the puck, where video doesn't record play development. It's all the little aspects away from the focus of the puck that scouts make note of. It's often those little things that make a player's career in the NHL.

"When video comes into play, I think it can supplement what your scouts do, but I don't think you can replace scouts—there's nothing like going to a game live. Watching

*a player from up above and away from the play and in
certain situations when the game changes, you can't sense
these little things when watching on a video. For example,
it's not whether a kid can skate or shoot the puck, it's some
of the little things that you can only pick up at a game.
There are certain things you can use from video scouting,
and we do use it to supplement what our scouts supply."*

Gretzky agrees that video has its drawbacks, including the
quality of the video being shot. In the end, though, he still
believes that having video is valuable.

*"The negative thing about video scouting is that it doesn't
show you everything, but at least it gives you some insight
when you watch the player. It really depends on the video,
sometimes you get good ones and other times it's not as
good, but anytime you can see more of a player it's a good
thing."*

Trevor Timmins is in full agreement with both Keith Gretzky
and Brent Flahr. He likes video scouting as a tool and thinks
it has a place in scouting, but says it can never replace live
viewings.

*"Well, I think it's another tool, but nothing replaces being
at a live game. You can see how the play develops and
what the player is doing away from the play that the
camera does not pick up. I think it's impossible to just rely
on video scouting, and it's just another tool to use to assess
player qualities."*

COMPUTER SOFTWARE

Back in the day, and I know a few scouts will remind me they're really not that old when I say that, all scouting reports and schedules were written by hand. The time required was enormous, and these tedious tasks had to be done on a daily basis. The norm was for scouts to take notes at the game (or to try to remember everything) and then head back to their homes or hotel rooms and write everything down on a form. These were triplicate forms, and one copy would be mailed out to the head scout, one to the team office, and the final one was kept by the scout for his reference and for use at scouting meetings. Trying to coordinate a scouting staff when the league schedules were issued on a photocopied sheet of paper was a tough task as well. The lack of instant communication and updates when it came to player injuries and other vital information made viewings hit and miss.

That all changed when *Jim Price* developed software to allow greater organization for the scouting departments. Little did he know how dramatically it would impact the industry. The software, called RinkNet, gives scouting departments a platform on which to organize all of the information they gather. This means that information is now instantly accessible to everyone in the organization. *Price* points out that some NHL teams were already using spreadsheets, but these programs were not hockey specific.

"When I started the company in 1998, most teams were already doing something. It wasn't overly coordinated; some teams had their own system that they had developed. Very few NHL teams were doing everything with three-ring

binders or that sort of a thing anymore. It might have been Excel spreadsheets or something else, but they were doing something. They knew the hockey business had gotten too big to keep it in their heads."

It was Jim Price's two backgrounds—hockey and computer programming—that helped launch an industry. His experience in the hockey industry had shown him how inefficient the current system was, and he used his computer expertise to develop a solution.

"They knew they needed help. I was able to come in having a hockey background, working in the OHL and with the Canadian Hockey League, and also a computer programming background and, you know, kind of married the two together. I jumped at the opportunity to get my first client. It's a small industry, everybody knows everybody, and word gets around quickly about that sort of a thing."

Jim Price

"Now, I wasn't around when the scouting departments didn't have RinkNet, but it's phenomenal as it's up to date and if you need anything it's right there. If you have any problems, they are a phone call away, and if you come up with an idea, RinkNet has been great about hearing it. I don't know how they did it in the old days. If you want to see a player or a game, all the information is a click away and the statistics don't lie. You know where all the games are and, with the scheduling, you know where your scouts are. It's a pretty good tool."

Keith Gretzky, Director of Amateur Scouting,
Phoenix Coyotes

Although *Price* and his staff appreciate any praise from teams and scouts, their goal was just to simplify and streamline things so the scouts could devote more time to finding new talent.

"I'm not going to say that our program has changed the world, but what we've allowed teams to do is to let the scouts, scout. It was all about 'let us worry about the background, the data, finding the information, schedules, and rosters, and that sort of a thing' and having a program that can organize it for the scouts. I don't think that we've changed things that much other than just allowing them to be more efficient and to use their time more effectively."

The scouts who use the software find it invaluable. How the scouting staffs use all the functions at their disposal depends on their needs, but with 29 out of 30 NHL teams currently using RinkNet on a daily basis, it has become a necessary tool of the trade.

Brent Flahr can't believe how the old guard organized their data and how RinkNet has changed that. Easily accessible data and up-to-date scheduling saves time and money for his staff.

"The scouting software has helped dramatically. At the beginning of scouting, guys would write stuff down on a card and sometimes fax it in or they did their list on a napkin. Now you have the RinkNet software and we use that. Not only are your reports on there and in the office, but we have a database with everyone's reports and updated information on everything from heights and weights to

minor hockey history and injuries and every detail on a player. The scheduling ability is helpful and there are many benefits; you can save a lot of money knowing that there's an injury and sending a scout elsewhere. Also, you can see player trends and different things like that. Some teams use it more than others, but we take it pretty seriously."

What *Trevor Timmins* really appreciates about the software is how much information is in one place, instantly available 24 hours a day, and the unique customization available for each NHL team.

"The RinkNet scouting system is the Cadillac of the scouting world, and there is so much information available at our fingertips. It improves the quality and efficiency of the work we do. The advantage of the software is it's completely customized for each individual team."

According to *Mike Futa*, the scouting software has changed the way scouts do their jobs because of three main factors: the player rating system, staff scheduling, and accountability. For him, the increased accountability from each scout makes for improved accuracy of the staff. For instance, gone are the days when scouts could say after the fact, 'Oh yeah, I really liked that guy,' when that really wasn't the case. RinkNet makes things more transparent and allows everyone on the staff to ask questions about every player, even if they have not seen them.

"I think RinkNet is a godsend. I think everybody uses it differently, and I know there is a video portion to it, but we don't use that. We use it more to pull a schedule together at

our fingertips and see where our colleagues are and to pull up schedules and all our reports. To be able to build your own state-of-the-art program with your own rating system and have it right in front of you is a godsend. With this software there is accountability for everything you write and say about a player. If you put him on a list, it's all recorded on the database and it's there. So you can't come back and say, 'I didn't have him there or I didn't say that about this guy,' because it is all there. The best thing about it is the accountability it brings and you get away from, 'I liked that guy and I had him there on the list,' and all that crap. Now, not everybody is going to be right or wrong all the time, but the accountability is always present, so if you are going to say something about a player it's going to be on record."

INDEPENDENT SCOUTING DEPARTMENTS

The rise of independent scouting departments in the late 1990s added a new dimension to the world of scouting and provided a voice for up-and-coming scouts. In the current marketplace, the likes of Red Line Report, North American Scouting Service, International Scouting Services, and McKeen's Hockey all serve a purpose in the industry. While their information is seldom used by NHL teams, their impact on the hockey fan base has been huge. For both fans and the media they have become a vital source of information on the next generation of players, and without them a vital aspect of marketing the game would be gone. In addition to the tremendous amount of information they provide to the fans and media, these independents also provide a valuable training ground for up-and-coming scouts.

Although some fans believe that these outlets are secondary scouting departments, this isn't the case. *Mike Futa* points out that, while he respects their hard work and effort, any information provided by these independents is used as cross-reference material only. Although, given the importance of making the right picks, any opportunity to receive extra information is a valuable one.

> *"Without naming them or being too critical, I think they are more useful for junior teams when it comes to finder lists for European drafts. But for us it would be a cross-reference only. I actually know some of the guys that work for independent scouting services, and I respect the fact they are making a living doing them, but for me they are just a cross-reference."*

The stakes in NHL scouting are simply too high for teams to rely on information that comes from third-party sources over which they have no quality control. Even though he knows that some people use these sources to balance opinions on players and offset any mistakes they might make, *Futa* cautions against this. He thinks it defeats the whole purpose of investing the time and money into having your own scouting staff.

> *"I have found them to be similar at times, but NHL lists are so far different from everyone else's lists it's crazy. If you spent your whole year putting together your own list and then all of a sudden you look up Central Scouting or Red Line Report or ISS and they have the players in a different order and it upsets you, you are in the wrong business. It's your list and your staff has put the effort into it, so stand*

by it. I know guys that do it and cross-reference and switch their lists around so they can be safe picks. Then when the player doesn't work out well they can say, 'I know we picked them there but look where Central, Red Line, and ISS put them.' Then you are not using it for the right reasons."

Brent Flahr says his team makes its decisions based on information gathered by its own scouts, but does admit that the independents can sometimes be useful in uncovering players from remote locations who are not on their lists. Since the players are now found all over North America and Europe, the scouts simply don't have the time to reach every location.

"We go exclusively by what our scouts put together in terms of our lists, but the value of those independant guys' lists is sometimes they do bring up a name in obscure areas. Sometimes it's right and sometimes it's not. We all have scouting staffs, but time is valuable and sometimes we can't allocate the time to check out everyone at every level. Sometimes they have a pretty wide spectrum and gather information that is useful for us."

One independent stands out from the rest, however, and that's NHL Central Scouting. Created in 1975 by former NHL general manager Jack Button, Central Scouting began as a service to the NHL clubs. They employ 29 scouts (both full-time and part-time) who are based in Toronto and in Europe, depending on their territory. The scouts primarily watch the CHL and the U.S. college and junior leagues. They offer valuable information to teams, including weekly player injury and player movement reports, video footage, and player ranking lists.

Perhaps the most valuable service they provide is their annual Combine. Prior to the annual NHL Draft, Central Scouting invites the top 100 prospects to Toronto to participate in medical and fitness testing and to meet with NHL teams interested in drafting them.

In *Keith Gretzky's* opinion, the other independent scouting operations aren't a particularly useful tool for scouting departments; however, he views NHL Central Scouting differently as he knows their criteria, work ethic, and accountability.

> *"It's just like video in that it's a tool. You try to keep up to where guys are rated, but everybody has a different opinion. I think NHL Central Scouting can be a useful tool in identifying players and making sure our guys see them. Those guys at NHL Central Scouting work extremely hard and they are just like they belong to a team."*

Trevor Timmins agrees that NHL Central Scouting is the one they can rely on.

> *"I think the only one that's used is NHL Central Scouting, and that helps us with the identification process. I don't think the independent scouting services are used very often; they're another media source."*

STATISTICAL ANALYSIS FOR HOCKEY

The use of mathematical formulas to improve results when projecting prospects has become more popular in the last few years, allowing scouting and hockey operations departments to pinpoint the true efficiency of every hockey player. No longer able to simply buy developed players due to the collective bargaining agreement, the importance of quality and up-to-date information has never been greater. While some teams have been slow to embrace the use of statistics, to generate long-term success in the world of professional hockey, teams have to use every tool available and be willing to think outside of the traditional models. These mathematical evaluations can help to pinpoint the most important factors in a player's ability to play at the NHL level.

Analysis of hockey statistics, which is similar to the saber-metrics program used in major league baseball, provides a comprehensive evaluation of each potential NHL draftee's history in efficiency. There are two main advantages to using statistics in hockey scouting: the entire department will spend less time and fewer financial resources tracking and evaluating the players who have a lower chance of playing at an NHL level and, with the subsequent smaller list of qualified prospects to evaluate, the scouting staff will be able to give a more detailed analysis on those players who remain on their radar.

Statistical analysis isn't just used for amateur scouting. It's also valuable during trade evaluations and free-agent signings. During the free-agent season, and especially approaching the NHL trade deadline, time is of the essence, and the hockey operations staff requires all possible information at their disposal. In the current environment, most transactions have multiple layers of NHL players, prospects, and draft choices. Receiving the highest value for each transaction is crucial, and adding another information source can make the difference between winning and losing. Statistics can be particularly useful in evaluating the efficiency of the organization's current players. Understanding which players will give the organization the greatest chance to succeed and which need to be moved to different organizations in exchange for other assets is paramount.

The value of hockey statistics has been debated since we began keeping them, but the important thing to remember when using them is to dig below the surface, as statistics can fool you if you take them at face value. For instance, a player scores 31 goals in his draft year. At first glance one would think he had a good year scoring goals, but how many of those goals actually directly impacted the game in a positive way? Other questions need to be asked as well, such as: what type of goal did he score? Did he score at home or away? Who was on the ice against him? Was he facing the top defensive pairing and the top checking line? How much ice time did he receive and what type of ice time in relation to the goals he scored?

Example of Statistical Analysis for Hockey

Consider the following basic examples to show the value of statistical analysis.

Jordan Eberle (2007–2008) Clutch Goal Scoring

In the 2007–2008 season, Jordan Eberle had 42 goals in 70 games. Teams need to determine how many of those goals impacted the outcome of the game and how many were inconsequential, such as the fifth goal in a 6-2 victory.

2007–2008 Statistical Data:

42 goals scored, 25 of which were clutch goals = 59.52 percent of Eberle's goals impacted the potential outcome of the game.

Final Conclusion:

Undervalued based on where he was drafted in the NHL.

Keep in mind that this is a very basic example, only showing a small glimpse of the potential of statistical analysis. Other important factors must also be considered, including: where, when, how, what team he was playing against, regular season vs. playoffs, and so on. The example below shows the importance of digging deeper.

Mitch Wahl (2007–2009) Clutch Goal Scoring

2007–2008:

20 goals scored, 7 of which were clutch goals = 35.0 percent of Wahl's goals impacted the potential outcome of the game. Now, the danger of not analyzing statistics fully and properly while also understanding the game of hockey can cause you to interpret the information incorrectly. In Wahl's case, he scored 7 of his 20 goals against Portland, with 5 of those goals being scored on home ice. During that season, Portland had a record of 11-52-2-1 for a winning percentage of .174. Clearly, not understanding or including the other factors can mislead you about how efficient a player actually is against the top competition.

2008–2009:

32 goals scored, 20 of which were clutch goals = 62.5 percent of Wahl's goals impacted the potential outcome of the game. Once again, the danger of not analyzing statistics fully while understanding the game of hockey can cause you to interpret the information incorrectly. In this season his numbers jumped dramatically, so scouts have to go back and ask why. What changed with him and his surrounding environment? The answers to these questions are what scouts try to find out when evaluating prospects year to year. All the statistics can lead scouts to look for the answers in a variety of places.

Use of statistics as a tool for hockey player evaluation has been growing slowly over the past few years. After Mike Futa joined the Los Angeles Kings, he began using statistics as a tool along with all the other data collected on a prospect. General Manager Dean Lombardi implemented the use of statistics as a tool within the entire hockey operations department. *Futa* thinks this was a good move and feels it allows the scouting department to see the prospect from a different perspective in terms of efficiency of ice time.

> *"He [Lombardi] has respect for the statistical side, even more so in the development side of the business, similar to how baseball uses it to assess developing skills. I don't know about other organizations, but the synergy in our organization and the ties between the draft and the development team and the statistical group are seamless."*

PART 2

Inside the Secret World of Hockey Scouting

CHAPTER 5

The Scouting Fraternity

"At a World Junior Tournament in Slovakia, I woke up New Year's Day with a pig's head on my pillow. Some rival scouts had taken the pig's head (apple still in its mouth) off the buffet table that night and got into my room when I was sleeping and deposited it on my pillow."

Marshall Johnston, Director of Professional Scouting,
Carolina Hurricanes

To understand any profession it's important to understand the people who do the job. For scouts, this is not simply a job or a career, but a lifestyle that they embrace. I'm not talking about the nuts and bolts and the day-to-day routine, but the relationships scouts have with each other. This provides the backdrop to all the players they draft. They are a unique band of characters who add colour to the world of hockey.

Like all sports, it's the stories of the people involved that is the fabric of the game of hockey, not the hype created on television sets. The scouting industry is similar to a covert international spy network. Imagine each NHL organization is a country and its scouting staff is a network of spies, each gathering valuable information and planting bad intelligence to keep the other spies away from an intended target. In spite of the competition, it's also a brotherhood that is surprisingly supportive. Nowhere is this more evident than when you hang around with scouts before a hockey game. One would think that the players they drafted and how their prospects performed the previous night would dominate the conversation. However, the complete opposite is true. In fact, the scouts' room is like a Friday night at a university frat house, with a constant barrage of stories, one-liners, and laughter that permeates the room. If you didn't know better, you might think it was a comedian convention.

LONG ROAD TRIPS AND BAD COFFEE

While fans generally see the glorious ending of the Stanley Cup final or the excitement and hope of the NHL Entry Draft, all the hours of work that go into making those great moments are decidedly less glorious and glamorous. With the recent emphasis on strong drafting and player development because of the salary cap, the word "scouting" has become sexy in the media. When I mentioned that observation to current NHL scouts, it was met with a heavy chorus of laughter. Then one of the older scouts, who looks like one of the old men who sit in the balcony on *The Muppet Show*, asked, "Why is everyone laughing? I am sexy!" Which, of course, was quickly followed by even more laughter.

If you really want to know what it's like to be an amateur scout, think about living out of a suitcase for 15 days of each month from September to the end of May. Then imagine driving all over hell's half acre in winter conditions at all times of the night and day, staying at crappy hotels, and eating road food day after day. Of course, you won't be seeing NHL games, but rather games in Swift Current, Saskatchewan, Val-d'Or, Quebec, or Owen Sound, Ontario, in the middle of winter. The truth is, to do this job you have to be either crazy about hockey or just plain crazy.

I'll let the scouts tell you in their own words, about the (not so) glamorous life on the road.

Bruce Haralson: Pro Scout, Detroit Red Wings

What I always find intriguing is how the average hockey fan looks upon scouting as this glorious job because we get to see hockey games every night and travel around the globe. I always get a chuckle out of it. To a degree they're right because it is exciting and everything else. But they forget about the times you get stuck in some little community in Russia somewhere, where the poverty level is below anything anyone over here in North America has ever seen.

On a road trip to Russia back in the early 1990s, it was so cold that we would set a bottle of water out onto the hotel room's windowsill and in the morning it would be frozen solid. You had to sleep in your clothes because the bed was so dirty, and in the morning you'd turn on the water in the shower and it was this kind of dirty-yellow colour and there were cockroaches running up and down the drain.

Then when you got on a flight to go to another stop in Russia, the stewardesses would come and you'd think, 'Great, we're going to get some service,' but all they did was cook themselves a meal and eat it. Then you see the guys de-ice the planes. In North America they use a machine. Over there you see a guy cleaning the wing with a mop and a bucket. You'd probably never get on a plane over here if you saw that. I remember on the same trip I got on a flight and this old Russian man gets on the plane carrying a 20-pound propane bottle and he sits it between his feet while we were looking at it like it was a ticking bomb. But I must admit, those things don't happen when the guys go over now.

Closer to home, I can remember one time I was travelling with Ken Schinkel and Greg Malone. We were driving back from Lake Placid, New York, and we were on the highway between Kingston and Belleville in Ontario. The road conditions were bad and it was snowing and a semi went by and we couldn't see the road. I mean we couldn't see anything; we were just blinded. Ken was driving and I was sitting in the passenger seat and Bugsy [Greg Malone] was in the back seat. Then Ken said, "I got the car straight," and I said, "To hell you do, you have to go right and we are going left." All of a sudden we go down into the ditch in between the two freeways. Our hearts were in our throats, but we came out of the ditch and back onto the freeway. Ken said, "We're okay now," and I said, "Like hell we are, we're going down the freeway in the wrong direction!"

About a half a mile down the road we could just barely see another semi-truck bearing down on us and I was freaking scared. There are those turning areas between the freeways for emergencies and we managed to use one to avoid the truck. We got back on the freeway, going in the right direction, just as the visibility started to clear up a little. We started back towards Belleville, and there was a culvert about 50 yards ahead of that access road. If we'd been any closer and hit that culvert, we'd have all been dead. After we'd been driving for about 10 minutes, we noticed that Bugsy in the back hadn't said a word. All of sudden he said, "I think I shit myself."

I have travelled halfway around the world scouting, and I'm lucky to be able to look back at all those great memories, even though some of them scared me half to death.

Jay Heinbuck: Director of Amateur Scouting, Pittsburgh Penguins

Everyone has horror stories about lost luggage. At the Under-18 World Junior Championships a couple of years ago, I remember a scout on our staff, Darryl Plandowski, lost his luggage on the way to Kazan, Russia. The poor guy would call the airline every day. And every day they would say it would be in tomorrow, so he wouldn't buy any clothes because his luggage was going to be there tomorrow. He kept calling, and they kept saying, "Tomorrow." This went about 10 days, and he was still wearing the same clothes. So on our staff he earned the nickname 'Skunky.' We all had a really good laugh at his expense, and he took it pretty well, considering.

Jim Hammett: Former NHL Scout

I remember one time Don Paarup and I were driving back from Calgary to Cranbrook, and midway through we hit the worst windstorm I have ever seen in my life. It was almost flipping the car over. We lucked out and managed to pull over to the side of the road and get to a gas station. Then Don decided it would be a good time to fill up the car with gas, even though the wind was blowing so hard we could barely open the car doors. He managed to open the door and get out. He was holding on to the car door handle with one hand and in the other hand he had the pump. Now, Don is a 6-foot-3 guy, but he let go of the door handle and the wind just picked him up and shot him out like a tumbleweed. I thought he was gone forever.

Seriously, I thought we'd lost him. People inside the gas station were watching this, and their eyes were as big as golf balls. I was completely freaking out and I couldn't see him, couldn't see him at all. I ended up putting the car in drive and moving it around the side of the building so it would act as a wind shield so I could get out of the car. I could barely move, but I crawled along the side of the wall to get into the gas station; it was like a *Seinfeld* episode. All of a sudden out of nowhere, Don comes out of this windstorm and he was absolutely fighting it as hard as he could. All those people in the gas station were trying to wave him in. I grabbed him by one hand and pulled him in the door. It was unbelievable.

At the time I was scared stiff because I thought I'd lost him and he has blowing all the way back to Calgary. You should have seen the looks on peoples' faces when Don got inside the gas station. They clearly just thought he was nuts; after all, there were 110 km or more winds and this guy tried to get out of his car to fill it up with gas.

HOCKEY HIJINKS

Remember at the beginning of the chapter when I mentioned that the scouts' room is sort of like a university frat house? Well, just like in a university fraternity, humour and practical jokes reign supreme in the scouting world. But the scouts who are the butts of the jokes shouldn't feel bad. When people spend that much time together at the rink and on the road, they become like family. The practical jokes are just a show of affection.

Here, in the scouts' own words, is a small sampling of the jokes that get played around the league.

Marty Stein: Amateur Scout, Detroit Red Wings

A few years back, I got a letter in the mail. It looked like a form and was a list of all the things a scout should be doing. Things like the way he looks and what time he should arrive at the rink, and so on. It had a list of all these scouts on there, and I got low marks, and Ernie Gare got some low marks on the way he dressed. It was quite the sheet, and everywhere we went scouts were asking, "Did you get that letter?" The other scouts said they got it, too, and after a few months we figured out it was Garth Malarchuk behind it. We carved him up pretty good after that. But he had us going, and it was a pretty good prank because the letter looked official with a company name and everything.

About three years ago, I went to Kamloops on a road trip, and Ernie Gare got this new phone. He kept saying, "Look at this phone, it can do this and it can that." He was all excited and then the phone rang and he didn't know how to answer the damn thing. So, of course, we got everyone to start phoning him, and eventually he figured it out. He was swearing at it, and we all had a good laugh.

Jim Hammett: Former NHL Scout

I was with Don Paarup at a game when I was working with Colorado. It was free haircut night at the game in Lethbridge. Now, Don decided that was the night to go get a haircut, and at the tail end of the haircut Garth Malarchuk walked up behind the girl cutting the hair. He said, "Give me the scissors," and took a big chunk of hair off the back of Don's head, but Don didn't figure it out until it was too late. He never got Garth back for that one, and Garth has gotten him a hundred times over.

I remember one time I was sitting beside Don at a Calgary Hitmen game. Traditionally I sit with Don and get myself a coffee and grab him a decaf and we watch the warm-up. Well, you know that Anbesol stuff you use for a toothache that makes everything numb? Well, I rubbed that on the outside of the rim of the coffee cup. I looked over about 10 minutes into the game and he was poking his chin, and 15 minutes in he was biting his lip and he couldn't figure out what the hell was going on. He must have been thinking he was having a heart attack or a stroke, and I was laughing so hard. The coffee was dribbling down his chin and it was perfect.

Although Don is the butt of many jokes, he loves it.

Scott Luce: Director of Amateur Scouting, Florida Panthers

The funniest thing I can recall is my first NHL Draft in 2000 with the Tampa Bay Lightning. It was Calgary's pick, and Barry MacKenzie had just made their selection in the first round. It was a very emotional speech that Barry had made, and after his time in the spotlight he came back from the podium towards the team tables. Our Draft tables were one in front of the other and he was so excited that he sat down at our table and said, "That was tougher than I thought it was going to be." He had sat down at the Tampa Bay Lightning table in General Manager Rick Dudley's chair. I said, "What the hell are you doing here?" really loud and kind of mad. I was actually kind of mad, because right in front of him was our list, and so I said, "Get the hell out of here, that is our GM's chair!" The Calgary Flames table was laughing and our table was laughing, but I wasn't laughing. Barry was all rattled and embarrassed at the time, but he had a good laugh about it later. I guess because I knew the value of having that list there, I took it a little too seriously. But it has always been one of those stories that the Calgary staff and the Tampa staff get a good laugh about.

Jim Nill: Assistant General Manager, Detroit Red Wings

Guy Lapointe, the famous Hall-of-Fame defenceman, and I were up in the Quebec league together and there were about 15 scouts there at that time. Guy is a real character and a real classy guy, and he always has something going on. The scouts are always buying the 50-50 draw tickets, and some of the scouts we were with didn't speak French. Guy happened to lean over and see John Stanton's numbers on his 50-50, so he wrote them down on his program in really small writing. They go to announce the 50-50 award winner and John didn't know what the numbers were because they were announced in French. So he said to Guy, "What were those numbers?" Guy looked at the numbers he had written down and said, "It's

44429." Then John says, "What were those numbers again?" and Guy repeats it and John says, "I won!" So Guy told him to go down by the penalty box to get his money. So John was all jacked up because he won the 50-50, but Guy had told him the wrong numbers and we all knew what was going on. So John went down by the penalty box and gave the guy his 50-50 ticket, but the guy kept saying "No, no, no, this is the wrong number." John kept arguing with him and we were all waving and laughing because Guy had set him up. There are always things going on like that; it really is a tight-knit group.

Mike Futa: Co-Director of Amateur Scouting, Los Angeles Kings

I know with our group of guys it's like having your own dressing room and you're playing again. I do think I have a better family group and the best staff I have ever been on. I don't think I've ever seen so much ball busting in my life. If you don't have a thick skin, you are dead with all the practical jokes and heat you take for every aspect of your life—your decisions, your reports, everything. As far as the other teams go, it's a fraternity. For example, me coming in as a young guy as an OHL manager, it took no time for me to fit in.

There are so many good people in the industry and I've become good friends with Keith Gretzky of the Phoenix Coyotes, and we have ongoing pranks with those guys. I remember two years ago at the NHL Draft our schedules crossed, so we knew which players they were meeting with and we knew they wanted defenceman Oliver Ekman-Larsson badly, like hugely.

We also knew that we wanted to take a forward, but nobody else knew that; they assumed but they didn't know for sure.

I remember we had the name bars written up for the prospects at the Draft. We saw Evander Kane went to Atlanta and I leaned back and took a deep breath. Then I just look to my right and Gretz [Keith Gretzky] looked at me and his eyes were burning through me and he gave me a look that said, "Who are you taking?" and I mouthed back to him "Ekman-Larsson." He just about fell off his chair and his whole face turned white and he began to sweat. We started to dig into the bag of name bars we had. We were taking Brayden Schenn all the way—if he was there, he was our guy. But it looked like the Coyotes staff was freaking out. Gretz told me later that they said, "I thought they were your friends," and "What the fuck?" At that time, I was shuffling through bag for the Ekman-Larsson name bar so I could pull that out to even add a little more pain.

When we announced Schenn you could see the load come off Keith's shoulders, and it was a little thing but it shows the humorous side. It shows you can go an entire year and the confidentiality factor is incredible. You can be the best friends in the world and go out for beers and wings and still nobody knows who's doing what. It's the best cone-of-silence bubble ever, and you never ask each other. You might say after a game, "So and so really sucked tonight," but nobody asks you about players and there is a respect factor about lists. Again when it comes to showtime, here we are at the last second before we have to pick and they still think we are taking Ekman-Larsson. It was a fun day, and I know Keith will never forgive me for it!

Garth Malarchuk: Amateur Scout, Toronto Maple Leafs

I've got a good Don Paarup story where we were in Lethbridge and they had a [hair-cutting] promotion. Brad Robinson and I snuck around and we were looking out on the ice and we crawled up the platform and took over and did a pretty good hack job on his hair.

In reference to the story about the letter rating all the Western scouts, I think that was my two friends Ernie Gare and Glen Dirk. I think that those two pricks were involved in that and I get blamed for it. Everybody points the finger at me for that one, but it was pretty funny. I remember them rating Darwin Bennett low on his dress code and giving him an up do. There were some feelings hurt on that one, but it wasn't me.

I remember one time, it was the year of the NHL strike so there were no overnight stays. We were going to Kamloops from Calgary, a six-hour drive, and then having to come back, so get four guys in the car and go to the game and take turns driving back cause there were no overnight stays. So we go to Kamloops and it's about 30°–40° below. Right away we always put Don Paarup in the front seat 'cause it'd give him a little more leg room, and as soon as we got in the car he's asleep, and you can just about do anything to him. Hey, once he's asleep, he's asleep. So Brad's driving and he pulls into Revelstoke and he's telling everybody in the car to be quiet. He puts it into neutral so that we coast into the gas station and we all get out, we turn the car off, take the keys out, we open the doors and Don is still sleeping. We go on and have a coffee and we are sitting there watching. He won't open his eyes but he's got his arms curled up and he's trying to get warm and he's reaching over for the heater but he won't open his eyes and he doesn't see that we aren't even there. So we came out about 10, 15 minutes later and he was covered in frost all over like he was frozen. I don't want to tell too many stories to embarrass guys like Don, as he is a real good friend.

Once we broke into another scout's room that I probably should not name and we put cellophane over his toilet. We unscrewed the light bulbs halfway so he couldn't turn the light on, and then we short-sheeted his bed and filled it up with shaving cream, and the story goes on and on.

Glen Dirk: Amateur Scout, New Jersey Devils

Like when Barclay Parneta came on the NHL scouting scene, working for Phoenix and then St. Louis. Barclay has provided a lot of entertainment for a lot of people simply because he's Barclay, and you can quote me on this. He was so excited, he was like a bride on her wedding night. I mean, I remember golfing with him at the Memorial Cup. We were out golfing and he let out a holler. I just about jumped out of the golf cart. I didn't know if we'd run over somebody that I didn't see or what had happened. And I said, "What the fuck is the matter with you?" and he said, "I can't believe it. I'm a scout in the National Hockey League and I am golfing all at once!" I said, "Really? Now that I've got my heart back in place, can we play the next hole?" I mean that's just Barclay, he's entertaining.

Dean Malkoc is one of the classiest people that I know and he gets more abuse than anybody, but it's very friendly.

I have never razzed anybody I didn't like. You're not necessarily being mean, but you bug them, and I bug them and get on their case because I like them.

Charlie Hodge is a class act, he belongs in a class all his own. He belongs at the head of the class, followed by Barclay and Malkoc. And he's been there. Great humour.

Well, like Paddy Ginnell. I don't like to bring his name up in a prank because he's passed on, but Garth Malarchuck pulled a great stunt on him once. Great guy and, you know, certainly missed big time when he passed on. I have to admit that his two sons have continued on in the business and they've maintained the same personality and at least are attempting to acquire the same respect that Paddy had. Respect is what you earn, and Paddy earned it. These guys will, too. They are still young but they will in the end because they are good people. That's Erin and Danny.

I know one time there was a big puddle in the road and all the cars were driving around it, but not Bob Brown. He decided he would drive through it, and when he stalled in the middle of it, the water was up to his waist. He had to get himself a new, well practically a new, car—a new engine and new everything. I think it was Barclay that hung a scuba mask and snorkel in the scouts' room for Brownie on his next trip. I thought that was pretty humorous.

And another time, when Bob Brown first started, he asked me for advice on how to be accepted as one of the guys. So I told him to stop into the coach's room to get the lines. "You know," I said, "that'd be a good start for you as a rookie." So anyway, he did it that time. Shortly after that he had a flat tire in the parking lot. So Gerry O'Flaherty and I put a note under the windshield wiper. It said, "all four will be flat next time if you don't get the lines, because you didn't get them tonight." Now it left him in doubt; he was trying to figure out, did they flatten it or didn't they?

I will tell you, when it comes to pranks there are three people I wouldn't trust at all, and Ernie Gare is one of them. Garth Malarchuk is another, and Gerry O'Flaherty is a classic in his own right. If you want to get set up, those three are very good, very, very good. You know George Fargher? Ernie used to pull some bad shit on him. George was innocent because he'd just started scouting at the time. You work with them all and you're on opposing teams, but you are never opposed in personality. There are some real classic people that will remain my friends for life.

Dan Ginnell: Amateur Scout, St. Louis Blues

Guy Lapointe is the biggest practical joker of all time and just a tremendous person, but he would just do little things to get at you. He and my dad would go for lunch, and my dad would get up and put his jacket on after lunch and his pockets would be full of sugar and salt, right to the top. He would dig his hand into his jacket and it's nothing but salt. Guy would do whatever he could do to lighten things up, he was unbelievable.

CHAPTER 6

Influential Scouts

"You know, guys just take care of each other out there. I think people who have been doing it a long time and are kind of connected to the game at a grassroots level are good people and they work hard."

Tom Kurvers

As a fan, you can look through the history of your respective team's draft lists and statistics, but what does that really tell you? It only tells you which players were selected. It doesn't give you an indication of what went into making those picks or the true origins of the history of scouting. The history and the art of scouting have passed from one generation of scouts to the next by word of mouth. The willingness of the older, more experienced scouts to help each other and to show the rookies the ropes ensures that the scouting profession lives on.

Originally I wanted to profile the 10 most influential scouts in the industry, but as I researched this, I discovered that the number of influential scouts was staggering. It was impossible to narrow it down to 10. A laundry list of gentlemen has made a direct impact on the quality of NHL teams and on the quality of the lives of other scouts, often with little fanfare or even acknowledgement from the average hockey fan. Ironically, if the fans out there were looking for someone in the NHL who they could truly identify with, it would most likely be a scout. They are a gang of regular guys who drink beer, bullshit, and have an immeasurable passion for hockey. Here is a partial list of scouts who have become stewards of the game and scouting mentors through their hard work and dedication:

- Neil Armstrong (Montreal Canadiens)
- Jack Bowman (Buffalo Sabres)
- Eddie Chadwick (Buffalo Sabres and Edmonton Oilers)
- Jack Davidson (Chicago Blackhawks)
- Cliff Fletcher (Atlanta, Calgary, Toronto, Phoenix)
- Barry Fraser (Edmonton Oilers)
- Jim Gregory (Toronto Maple Leafs and NHL Central Scouting)
- Ian McKenzie (Calgary Flames)
- Ted O'Connor (Los Angeles Kings)
- Bob Owen (Atlanta Thrashers)
- Lou Passador (New York Rangers)
- Mike Penny (Toronto Maple Leafs)
- Doug Robinson (Montreal Canadiens)
- Murray "Torchy" Schell (Toronto Maple Leafs)
- Red Sullivan (New York Rangers)

- Billy Taylor (Washington and Philadelphia)
- Barry Trapp (Toronto Maple Leafs, Hockey Canada)
- Jimmy Walker (Chicago Blackhawks)
- Del Wilson (Scouted from 1949–1995)

To find out who some of the other key figures are in the scouting world, I figured it made sense to ask the men in the trenches. Below, some of today's influential scouts tell us about their own mentors and the influences these men had on them and on the success and direction of hockey scouting.

JACK BUTTON, SCOUTING MENTOR

Well, I think that a big part of it was that your parents influence you in so many different ways. I think that, outside of hockey, the influence he had on me was in terms of respecting people, listening to people, and giving people an opportunity. Those types of things are going to be with me forever.

I think he was really an open-minded guy. I mean you hear a lot of times different people talk about how he loved a good argument. But what he loved more than a good argument was somebody that was ready to engage in a good argument with him. It wasn't necessarily about him being right or wrong; it was more an interest in engaging and hearing what others had to say. So I think from a personal standpoint those are qualities and characteristics that I think will always be a part of me.

He was always really, really open to ways to be better and to new people. I think he really demonstrated that when he worked with NHL Central Scouting. He started Central Scouting, and obviously we know the impact that Central Scouting has had and how people use it. But, you know, that builds from him to Jim Gregory, to Frank Bonello, to E.J. Maguire. They are wonderful, wonderful people that are not only passionate about scouting, but that are caretakers of the scouting fraternity. You know they want to make sure that the teams have the best information, the most information.

Craig Button

• • •

You know what the neatest thing about that was? When you're a kid, nobody wants to be a scout, right? You grow up dreaming of playing in the NHL and being a player. But you know what? Just watching him work day to day and seeing how he organized things and how thorough he was inspired me. I got to go to games and see how he interacted with other scouts and agents and talked to players.

The two things I can say would be: he was honest and upfront with you and he had great organizational skills. He didn't miss a beat, and he was very thorough in his organization. Those two things were probably the most prevalent that you take with you. You know, they weren't scouting lessons, they were life lessons. You could apply them in any aspect: in schooling or in any job you have. It translated directly into scouting now, but at the time you never knew where it was going to take you.

When I started travelling and scouting and meeting these guys, I heard stories all the time. Guy Lapointe and other scouts would tell me stories about him and how great he treated them. That kind of stuff really means something to the guys.

Tod Button

• • •

Well, I worked for Jack. When you worked for Jack, you'd better know where you were going. Jack Button was the most organized person that I have ever met in the hockey industry. He was very, very punctual and he expected you to do the same thing and he expected accountability, and that's all you can ask. I mean, it's your job to provide that, that's why he gave you the job, and I respected him tremendously. I mean we had our disagreements, but he wanted to make sure that what I felt and what I told him was what I actually believed. He wanted to know I wasn't going to be swayed and he respected that. If you had an opinion, you lived it right, wrong, or otherwise, and he respected that because that's exactly what he wanted. That's the way it should be.

Jack Button was very good. I think he had all the intelligence, all the smarts . . . he was very, very capable. I worked with him for years in the past and he was very, very smart and very good at what he does. A good man, a good hockey man.

Glen Dirk

PADDY GINNELL, SCOUTING MENTOR

Obviously my dad was a tremendous influence. You know, coming from a hockey family growing up in Flin Flon when he was the coach of the Flin Flon Bombers we were always his sidekicks. Then, after my dad's coaching career, he scouted for the St. Louis Blues for 20 years. Unofficially, I was by his side for a lot of that time, discussing players and scheduling, and so it was a tremendous influence. He was a huge influence with experiences that he had and the people that he associated with, and the experience was invaluable. It's been terrific and these are great people who have great insight into the game.

I came in with the Blues in 2003, the year my dad got cancer. I owe everything to Larry Pleau for hiring me. You know, my dad was sick and he hired me to help my dad that year. Things have evolved from that point, but Larry is probably the greatest man in all of sport, and many people would tell you that.

Dan Ginnell

● ● ●

I was really lucky to get hooked up with Paddy, and of course Teddy Hampson was there, too. So right away we hit it off great. He's usually laid back, but when he got excited, he got really excited. He was always excited for the players we were going to draft and who were coming to the Blues. You know, he loved Western guys, but he'd look at everybody the same. If they were a player and he liked the way they competed and played, he liked them. I learned that it doesn't really matter where you come from, it just matters how you play and what kind of guy you are.

He was willing to help everybody and he was a great guy to everybody. He was one of the guys that I miss all the time. I was lucky to be able to work with him. Even the guys that he touched outside of the Blues organization had a lot of respect for him because he did his job and he said what he thought. He wasn't one of those guys who thought it was his way or his player, it was always just about the player and about everybody else. In fact, I just like Paddy for the way he was; he was honest and sincere and I like to think we came from the same mould. He's just a friend to everybody, and that was the good thing about Paddy—everybody was a friend.

Mike Antonovich

JOHN FERGUSON SR., SCOUTING MENTOR

My dad was obviously very influential on me in many ways. I grew up around the game, really at the tail end of his playing career, and then after that throughout his managerial career and on to his role as a director of player personnel and pro scouting. I remember his willingness to do what he called "his homework," which was go where he needed to go to watch players play. He understood not just the importance of being able to project how that player might be in two, three, four, five, 10 years, but also the work that goes into it and the benefits of working smart and outworking your competitors. He prided himself on that and the proof is really in the pudding. But you know, he has been able to not only identify players drafted high, but to identify some stars drafted late. I think he earned a great deal of respect for that, and deservedly so. All of that left a tremendous positive influence on me personally. I mean, we could go on and on about his influence and his reach, and it's not just scouts that benefitted from that important counsel.

John Ferguson Jr.

* * *

I would say John Ferguson Sr. had the biggest impact on my scouting career. I had retired from playing and was coaching down in Glen Falls.

That was before Ottawa had a franchise, so we were doing some scouting for the Expansion Draft, and the following year they got the franchise. They got John on board, and I knew John from the Winnipeg days when I played for him. He was just a highly respected man. I got to work with him on the scouting end of things, and he had such a tremendous impact on me. Here was John Ferguson, the tough, big, snarly winger of the Montreal Canadiens days, and to watch him in the scouting world was great. He loved skill and something he always talked to me about was that your players have to have lots of skill. He always told me character was important too, and not to overlook it. He was the one who made a difference to me, and we drafted Pavol Demitra and Daniel Alfredsson in Ottawa, and those were later picks. John not only impacted me as a scout, but as a person as well. He was a real sincere person, loyal and accountable, and just a great man overall.

Jim Nill

MARSHALL JOHNSTON, SCOUTING MENTOR

For me it was Marshall Johnston definitely, because that was my first boss. He was very diligent. I mean the guy was very thorough, had a lot of patience, he was very good with younger players. He always seemed patient and wise, never impulsive. He had a lot of good qualities. I think that's why he was so good for so long with so many teams.

To give you an example, Marshall is the kind of guy that wants no credit. He would throw a Christmas party at his house in New Jersey, and he invited everybody in the office. He had a relationship with everybody, and that's the reason why his scouts stayed with him for so long. Just say there is guy making $60,000 and there is a guy making $5,000 as a part-timer, he will literally listen to them both the same. There is no like 'oh this is my full-time guy so I will listen to him,' so everybody was a part of it and everybody got their say. His belief in drafting and developing and his nurturing of younger players was unbelievable. Anybody that ever worked for Marshall Johnston would say he put everybody else before him; they would all say that. His people would go to war for him.

Tim Burke

● ● ●

I would say Marshall Johnston was influential for sure. He was in charge of the New Jersey Devils draft at the time when I was drafted. He obviously is still involved in the game as director of player personnel in Carolina. He spent a fair bit of time with me and was a contact person through my junior career and into minor pro and pro playing days. Specifically when it comes to scouting, I have had conversations with him and he would remind me that there's no exact science when you are dealing with 18-year-old kids, although everyone wishes there was. We all have to go back to when we were 18 and remember what we were like, and there is certainly no exact formula that you go by. He is a guy that has done a lot of different things in hockey: heading up an NHL Draft table, pro scouting, and he's been director of player personnel and a general manager. Now he has a number of areas he can talk about with experience, which is unique.

Craig Billington

FRANK BONELLO, SCOUTING MENTOR

Yeah, I think there were a lot of guys that made you feel part of it even though you were just the young guy and they had been at it for a long time. Obviously, Frank Bonello, who hired me, was a big influence on me. Guys like Frank Bonello, Red Sullivan, and Doug Robinson certainly showed me how to navigate the business. They teach you how to carry yourself and that. I think that is a big part of it. Doug Robinson, Dave Lucas, Red Sullivan, and Frank Bonello, guys like that were so friendly and just kind of showed me respect.

Tim Bernhardt

● ● ●

When I broke into scouting, Frank Bonello gave me my first chance and helped me out a lot in that regard as well. You sure remember the guys that extended a helping hand out to you and didn't turn their back on you and helped you with the little things. To be honest with you, I had a lot of guys that helped me, but Frank Bonello is a name that really jumped out for me.

Jim Hammett

BART BRADLEY, SCOUTING MENTOR

I go back to when I was a little tyke, when I was five years old and my dad was scouting in the late '60s and early '70s. I followed his career all the way, and I happened to get into scouting myself and was fortunate to work with him for three years, learning the ropes with him. He was my hero and I learned so much. He always talked about the five S's and I actually added two more S's. You asked, "What do we scouts look for?" Well, sense, skating, skill, shooting, spirit, and you can throw in strength and size, too.

The lessons came full circle since my dad was involved in the Cam Neely trade in Boston and he possessed all the S's, and I drafted Milan Lucic, a similar player in many respects. It was gratifying, and there were several articles written on that subject, with my father being an integral part of the Cam Neely deal and myself running the Draft table and Milan being from Vancouver, as was Cam. My dad is not here anymore, but he would be very proud of that pick, and I think he has had a lot to do with my success in the business. Spending a lot of hours with him at games and, following my junior career, you meet guys like Marshall Johnston [who scouted] when there were only two scouts per team and they did it all—the amateur and the professional ranks. So there is a wealth of experience coming from scouts about the game and the fraternity, and you cannot learn enough from those guys.

Scott Bradley

LUKE WILLIAMS, SCOUTING MENTOR

He was a huge influence on me. I started off when I was around 21 or 22 and I was an assistant coach with the London Knights for a bit. I remember telling my friends that my dad leaves the house early in the morning and he is going to all the games while working in junior hockey and I could never see myself doing that. Then by the end of that year I did go to one tournament with him in Toronto over Christmastime, and after that I just seemed to keep going to games with him. When he was in the Soo, he asked me if I wanted to be a part of it, so I thought I would give it a try. It went on from there. It was something that I grew up with, and as I look back and I think about it, I was actually a scout long before I actually realized it.

I think I learned a lot from him in terms of how to respect people. He always had contacts that would help him and he treated them well and showed appreciation. I also think because we travelled so much when we worked together for the Soo Greyhounds that every trip was a meeting. We'd be driving to London from Toronto and back, and we'd have a little meeting for hours and talk about players and what I thought and what he thought. He was also open to what other people had to say, and you know I played for him and so I know what type of players he likes. I guess we like similar players to a degree, but there are also some differences and to talk to him about those things was fun. He always taught me to be respectful and listen to other people's opinions and hear what they have to say because you can always learn something. Now, it might not always be from a positive standpoint, but he said you would always learn something from someone.

John Williams

LORNE DAVIS, SCOUTING MENTOR

I was indoctrinated into the industry by the time I was born so, to be honest, I did not quite realize how much it really impacted me since it was almost like second nature to me. With me, and what many others have told me is, my dad never told you the answers but put you on the path to find the answers for yourself. He thought it was important to make your own mistakes and your own judgments.

He had a great knowledge and knew that he was not always right, and this job can be very humbling at times. Everyone will know you for the one great player that you found, but a lot of us have our names on a few skeletons in our closet, too, and my dad was the first to admit that. He never wanted to say that he knew everything, and he just wanted to help and show you this is the path to find good players. He had a great demeanor when he was talking to people and was never condescending. It didn't matter if you were an usher at a game or a first-year scout or a fan, he would listen to you as if you had something to say and he could learn something as much as he was giving back. That he was a good listener was something that endeared him to everybody.

I have been in those wars as a scout when you are battling and battling for your guy. We sometimes forget to listen when we are debating and start arguing to score points. Yet my dad would stop in the middle of the meeting and the argument and, even if it was against his player, he'd say, "What a great point you made." He would say, "I never saw it that way," and so it proved to me that he was not just the oldest and most experienced scout, he was the smartest in the way that he would always consider a different perspective and not accept things as absolute. He knew that you did not have to have played in the NHL or coached at a high level—everybody knows a little about this game.

Brad Davis

DON LUCE, SCOUTING MENTOR

When my father's career transitioned from player to scout to management, I was at an impressionable age, in my late teens and early 20s. He was very much a factor in regards to helping me see the light at the end of the tunnel—just because you are done playing does not mean you are done with the game. There are other opportunities within the game, and at a young age I took a very keen interest in the scouting side of it. Jack Bowman and my father were kind enough to let me be an apprentice scout for them when I was in my early 20s. So I went to over 100 games for them as a 22- and 23-year-old young man trying to get into the scouting fraternity, as we like to call it. At that time, in the early '90s, there were not many opportunities for young scouts. But my father was a strong influence and helped guide me in the right direction in regards to learning how to become a scout. I think people sometimes don't understand that there is a learning curve with being a scout.

Scott Luce

LOU JANKOWSKI, SCOUTING MENTOR

Well, growing up and going to the rink with Dad was when you got to spend time with him in the winter. I loved going to the rink with him and watching him do his thing because #1: I had a love of hockey just because Dad does what he does, and #2: I got to spend time with him.

He influenced me in everything. I mean you grow up watching him interact with coaches and GMs of junior teams, of NHL teams, and with other scouts in the business. I remember the relationships he had with people, the way he handled situations, the way he worked in the business, his understanding of the business—I just watched it all. We never had unbelievable discussions about hockey when I was growing up, but I saw everything that he did and how he handled everything and that is certainly 100 percent where I got my abilities.

His influence wasn't just on me, but on a lot of the next generation. That's one thing that came out when my father passed away a few months ago. David Conte and that group really supported our family with an outpouring of emotion and support after my dad's passing. They all said that Dad really helped them when they first started in the business.

Ryan Jankowski

RICK DUDLEY, SCOUTING MENTOR

I was fortunate enough to be hired by Rick Dudley, my first GM. He gave me my first job in the NHL as a scout. He was very helpful in my scouting career because he did a very good job as a general manager, helping his staff and identifying the key characteristics. He, as a leader of an organization, wanted to bring [assets] into the organization, so he was very good at breaking down prospects on their skill set basis and that gets you thinking as a scout. Rick Dudley would have to be the most influential guy outside of my father in regards to helping me with my pro hockey scouting career. Anytime someone gets the time to pick his brain it's time well spent because he has a real unique approach to it, and he does not waver from that. I think that is the thing with scouting, there is a lot of flip-flopping going on, but Duds sticks with his approach. He builds his book, as he likes to call it, from the start of the year to the end of the year, and he and his staff will make their decisions accordingly.

Scott Luce

GERRY MELYNK, SCOUTING MENTOR

The first time I met Gerry Melynk was in the '81–'82 season. I was playing for the Maine Mariners. My first European amateur scouting trip was to a small town in northern Finland called Jyvaskyla. The vets told me that flying overnight and going to two games is hard, so don't go to bed until after the games so your body clock can adjust easier. I had four hours until the first game started, and I could not stay out of my bed, so I slept for three hours. Needless to say, I watched both games and then lay wide awake, finally going down-stairs to the hotel lobby. Gerry and Craig Button were in the lobby having a beer, saw me, and said, "Can't sleep either?" The second time I met Gerry, they asked me to join them across the street for a late-night cheeseburger and I accepted. The two of them obviously had a close relationship, and they are both comedians. They took turns ripping off jokes into the wee hours of the morning, when sleep finally took over. My side ached from laughing when I woke up!

I'll let the drafting speak for itself on how good Gerry was as a scout, but what I do know from being in the very competitive fraternity of scouting, I cannot remember anybody ever saying a bad word about him.

Gordie Clarke

PIERRE DORION SR., SCOUTING MENTOR

The first guy I worked for was Pierre Dorion Sr. He was a huge influence on me. He'd come out of NHL Central Scouting and I learned a ton about the business from him, but everybody was really good. He was a guy that, you know, went out of his way and came up to you and said, "Look, hey, if you need a ride ..." or "Do you need anything?" or "If you need to know anything about where the rinks are or getting around or as far as organizing, don't be afraid to give me a call." All the older guys that had been around for a long time were the same way. It was like they went out of their way to make sure you felt like one of the guys.

Garth Malarchuk

ADDITIONAL INFLUENTIAL SCOUTS

Absolutely Charlie Hodge would be one. You know, whenever I would go out West he would show me around the interior of B.C. Lou Jankowski, who was working at the time, I believe, for the New York Rangers, and Doug Robinson, who was working for the Montreal Canadiens. Doug Armstrong's dad was tremendous to me when he was a scout for the Canadiens, and Jack Bowman, Scotty Bowman's brother, had a huge influence on me. These were older gentlemen who had been scouting for very long periods of time, and they taught me little tricks of the trade. You know, about how to travel wisely, what hotels to stay in that would be very friendly towards scouts. When travelling to Europe, they told you the countries where you would need a visa, countries where you didn't, and where to stay over there. These guys were good contacts in terms of getting you around, finding drivers, and things like that. So these were all gentlemen who were all extremely, extremely helpful to me.

Pierre McGuire

● ● ●

I will never forget Ace Bailey. When I started in the business and I was in a hockey rink, somebody must have pointed out to him that I was just starting out. I was working for Quebec and he went out of his way to come over and introduce himself, and he gave me his phone number and told me anytime I had a question or needed anything to call him. I always remember Neil Armstrong, Doug's father—the old referee, and he was scouting for Montreal. He was always a class act to me. I will tell you I worked for Quebec for five or six years and then I was hired by Pittsburgh to work over in Europe, and I always knew I was in the right rink and I was on the right track because I would run into Jack Button. If I saw Jack there, I knew I was close and was hoping I would find the right player because I was in the right place. The other guy I have is Barry Fraser. I knew Barry a little bit from scouting in North America. When I went over to Europe the first time it was a November tournament and Barry thought it was great that I went over there to live in Russia and scout in Europe. I remember we sat down two different nights and we just talked about European hockey.

Mark Kelley

• • •

I remember my first trip out to Ontario. I had told Darwin Bennett I was going to Ontario and he asked if it was my first trip out there. I told him it was and I was really excited about it. Well, he had gone out to Ontario earlier, so he dropped by my house and gave me the directions to every rink in the OHL—hand written. I don't know how he did it because this was way before we used the Internet and MapQuest. It was unbelievable, but that was how the older scouts were, and they did a really good job of making sure you were included and a part of the fraternity.

When I first started in Vancouver, I had Pat Quinn, who was the president, GM, and coach; Brian Burke, who was the assistant GM; and then George McPhee, who was the assistant GM after Brian moved on. What a great way to get started. I had Mike Penny as the head scout and Ron Delorme, and I was part-time but I never felt it, and those people were so good to me. They taught me so much and I was really fortunate I got off to the right start. As far as scouting, the people I worked for and a lot of the older scouts I mentioned really helped you out. I have been spoiled by the people I first worked with and those older members of the scouting fraternity because they were really great scouts and even greater people.

Ross Mahoney

PART 3

How to Tell
Who's Got Game

CHAPTER 7

Hockey Sense

"He has to quickly see what is there and make the play. It's an art, and it's not an easy thing to do."

Rick Dudley, General Manager, Atlanta Thrashers

Sit in the stands at any NHL game and you'll hear a fan say something like this, "How did that guy know to do that at exactly the right time?" And that is the essence of hockey sense. It's the capacity to process information while playing at speed and under duress. But what does that mean to the scouts who are trying to evaluate it? Because it's an intangible skill, every scout will have a slightly different interpretation. Here three scouts give their interpretation of hockey sense:

"Hockey sense: it comes down to he always seems to be around the puck or, better yet, the puck seems to follow him."

E.J. McGuire, Director, NHL Central Scouting

"Decision-making with the puck, that's hockey sense, and that is perhaps the most difficult skill to recognize. It is a God-given talent, and exceptional hockey sense is hard to find, so when you are rating it you have to take into consideration: his instincts, how he sees the ice and feels the ice, his ability to limit his mistakes, when he is thinking on the ice, and his anticipation."

Scott Bradley, Director of Player Personnel,
Boston Bruins

"The prospects that you are really trying to assess are the players that can see what is unfolding really quickly. Then being able to translate it quickly from their head to their hands and make the play—you can call that hockey sense."

Craig Button, Former NHL General Manager

Even though it's challenging to pinpoint exactly what hockey sense is, it's important for scouts to assess it, because one of the main reasons prospects fail to become consistent NHL players is that they lack hockey sense. The history of the NHL Draft has proven that the prospects with the greatest hockey sense have the greatest chance of succeeding. For example, Ryan Smyth and Corey Perry may not be the fastest skaters, but their hockey sense makes them quality players.

"Without good hockey sense or awareness, your other skills don't matter, and that's why so many players that can skate and have elements of skill do not succeed. It's not because they don't have the skill, it's because they don't have the intelligence."

Craig Button

Perhaps the best, and most recognizable, example of a player with great hockey sense is Wayne Gretzky, whose ability to always be around the puck was legendary. Current players who fit that mould include Sidney Crosby and Zach Parise, who always seem to be in the right place at the right time.

"The poster boy for this is Wayne Gretzky, who is always one or two chess moves ahead of the play."

E.J. McGuire

Tim Burke thinks Peter Forsberg and Sidney Crosby demonstrate good hockey sense. He's impressed with their abilities to out-think the opposition, to avoid being predictable, and to take advantage of opportunities when they present themselves. Not that scouts expect the prospects to be as good as these All-Stars, but ideally they should have a capacity to process information, because it will make them better decision-makers.

According to *Gordie Clark*, hockey sense has become even more of a priority for scouts and NHL teams since the rule changes in the 2005–2006 season. Now that defenders cannot cause interference by clutching and holding, less time and space is available on the ice. Finding players with the ability to make instant decisions about how best to use that time and space is important.

"... the NHL has changed the rules to allow the skilled players to play the game. So finding skilled players that can make the correct decisions at the right time is tough, and if you think you have found one of those, you focus and key on him."

Hockey sense is perhaps the most difficult hockey skill for scouts to assess. They could sit a room and debate how to evaluate it for days and never come to a consensus. However, if you look carefully, there are clues that separate one player from another. *E.J. McGuire* looks for prospects with the ability to orchestrate the chaos in front of them.

> *"The type of decision-making a player uses on the ice and the capacity to sort out the choices is only the first part. Then it's the ability to skate down the ice with his head up, dish the puck, and then go to an open area."*

Poise is a key sign of hockey sense in a prospect says Tony MacDonald, Director of Amateur Scouting, Carolina Hurricanes. Scouts need to watch the prospects to ensure they display poise with the puck and don't panic when threatened or under pressure. *MacDonald* also pays attention to the ability to read and instantly react to whatever opportunities arise.

> *"[We look for] the players that are patient, with a low panic point, and who try not to force the puck into coverage and take what the defence gives them. Also, if they are able to make a play and move the puck to good spots, that shows hockey sense. The players that can find open ice, read and react, and make decisions with the puck are vital."*

Marty Stein, Amateur Scout, Detroit Red Wings, agrees, adding that a prospect's confidence plays a major part in hockey sense.

> *"This is where his confidence level comes into play, as if you see a player who has the puck a lot and makes the right*

decisions most of the time, he is going to gain confidence . . .
which leads to the poise. Once he has that level of poise,
the player will become more creative. The more creative
he is, the more chances he takes with the puck, and that
leads to scoring chances. I think it really comes down to
confidence."

Tim Burke searches for players who are able to avoid getting
shut down offensively, to adapt depending on the circumstances, and to find creative ways to exploit the opposition.

"When it comes to hockey sense, the prospects can some-
times make plays in certain games and with certain players.
But the excellent ones that can process the game do not get
shut down, and if they do for a few shifts, they adjust and
may go to the other side of the rink and attack a different
part of the ice."

Although forwards and defencemen have different responsibilities and see the game from different perspectives, both
need hockey sense in abundance. Here's how *Rick Dudley*
contrasts the hockey sense needed for each position:

"A scout is looking to see if the forward can take the puck
on the wall, quickly see the best available option, and hit
him with the pass."

"It is paramount that the defenceman going back to retrieve
a puck surveys the ice on his way back. Second, can he
take the puck under the pressure of being hit and can
he immediately find the best available choice—without
having to look for it and without having to try a 50/50 pass
through a stick or something?"

Scouts also look to see whether prospects can anticipate and make the correct decision to create a scoring chance. It can be useful to watch for this skill in certain game situations, in particular in five-on-five situations where the opposition has been exposed and caught defending an odd-man scoring chance. For example, a defenceman who creates an odd-man opportunity by turning the puck over when he rushed it up the ice instead of passing it to an open forward demonstrated poor hockey sense. In contrast, a forward who takes advantage of the opportunity by recognizing the developing play in the offensive zone and finds the space to create offense demonstrates good hockey sense.

Man-advantage situations also provide a good opportunity for players to demonstrate their hockey sense. Former NHL scout *Harkie Singh* closely watches a three-on-two offensive rush for clues.

> *"For example, on a three-on-two situation, the prospect can give the scouts some significant clues. Which player stays high, which one drives to the net, which one drives the defencemen back on their heels? And of those players, which consistently makes the best decision the quickest?"*

Gordie Clark pays attention to two-on-one advantages.

> *"On a two-on-one, does the forward with the puck keep his head on a swivel, looking to set up his linemate while reading the defenceman? Does he look at the goalie to see if he's cheating and then make an instant decision once he sees the opportunity? I watch if the forward knows how to read a defenceman's stick and whether it is in the*

passing lanes or, if they are in an offensive situation, which way their toe caps are facing. Does the prospect give the impression of where they are passing the puck and does the whole building know where the puck is going?"

Now, you'd think that an elite-level prospect would know what to do and how to do it quickly, after all, his choices are limited—either hold, shoot, or pass. However, the pressure of the moment can cause players to make bad decisions. *Jay Heinbuck*, Director of Amateur Scouting, Pittsburgh Penguins, explains what he looks at:

"You look at the situation. If it's a forward and they are in a position to shoot or pass, are they in the scoring area? Also, is it a two-on-one or a three-on-two? If he shoots and scores or forces the goaltender to make a good save, that was a good decision. Conversely, if he hits the goalie and it was too easy, then maybe it was not so good. The other aspect is if he passed the puck and was able to thread it through for a scoring chance; if not, then he should have shot the puck instead."

Hockey sense isn't limited to what the prospects do, it also shows through in what they don't do.

"Hockey sense involves having an awareness of the game. Does he take a retaliatory slashing penalty? If, for example, he does and it's the third period with his team trailing by a goal, you would assume the player does not have a good awareness of what it takes to win."

Jeff Gorton, Assistant Director of Player Personnel,
New York Rangers

Scouts who are evaluating hockey sense also need to have an understanding of the system the prospect is playing under. Sometimes all the scout sees is the prospect making a bad decision, but if he was following his coach's instructions, then the decision isn't really a reflection of his innate hockey sense. Scouts must try to take the circumstances into account.

> *"A scout at a game has the challenge of trying to interpret the system the coach is asking a player to play. In other words, prospects might be under orders to shoot first and look for the pass later. We scouts are not privy to that and when we are evaluating we can fall into a trap. For example, if a prospect has his head down and is looking at the goal while his two linemates were a little more open, does that make him selfish? In a black-and-white world, the answer would be yes. But in a world that takes into account some instruction from a coach between periods or before the game, it is clearly no!"*

> E.J. McGuire

Scouts must predict if the prospects have (or will have) the maturity to make decisions that benefit their teams. But the development of maturity is tricky to project accurately. While other hockey skills develop in a linear way, maturity is less predictable. As a result, projections regarding hockey sense will be less exact than those of the other skills.

SCOUTING SCORECARD

❑ Is the prospect poised and confident?

❑ Is he patient?

❑ Is he able to find the open ice?

❑ Does he see opportunities and take advantage of them?

❑ Does he choose the best options available to him when he's under duress?

❑ Does he display game sense (i.e., avoids needless penalties)?

❑ Can he react to situations and adjust his play accordingly?

CHAPTER 8

Skating

"Boy, if we all had the 100 percent answer on skating, we could make a lot of money because one of the hardest parts is trying to project skating ability, especially if a guy's stride is a little flawed. How are we going to determine if it's going to get a little better?"

Jay Heinbuck, Director of Amateur Scouting,
Pittsburgh Penguins

The differences between a bad skater and a good skater are like night and day, but breaking down each individual part of a player's skating ability can be tricky. Fans can easily spot the difference between the speed demon racing around the juniors and the player who skates like he has a piano tied to his ass. But they're often left scratching their heads when the slow player makes it to the NHL, so the question is: How does that happen? It can happen for a couple of different reasons. For example, *Scott Bradley* notes that scouts ranked Kyle Wellwood as a below-average skater when he was a junior, but he still made it to the NHL because of the value of his other skill sets:

> *"You take a Kyle Wellwood and look at his skating. He plays in the NHL, but he might be a below-average skater and so why is he playing? If he's not a great skater or not even an average skater, then he's playing because he has great hands, knowledge of the game, and hockey sense."*

Other players make it to the NHL because while their skating may not be the best overall, there are particular situations in which it does excel. *Tim Burke* notes:

> *"You look at a guy like Pavel Datsyuk, for example. People will say he is a good skater, not a great skater. But when he is in a race for the puck, he ends up there first. Dany Heatley is another one that is not considered the fastest on the ice, but he's beating people to the puck as well. Some guys are faster with the puck than without it. Which is better? A scout has to gauge different situations—the prospect skating with the puck and without."*

Obviously, evaluating skating is not as simplistic as some hockey fans believe. *Jeff Gorton* points out the basics:

> *"There are a lot of theories on what makes a good skater, including a wide track and a long stride. There also are certain types of skaters you are trying to stay away from, like those knock-kneed skaters or short-stride guys."*

Unfortunately, analyzing skating is an inexact science, and sometimes scouts make mistakes when trying to project prospects, writing off players who end up being successful. *Gorton* explains:

> *"But at the same time, when some of the best players in the NHL were still prospects we scouts were saying that their skating will hold them back. Most of the better players found a way to improve their skating. As scouts we want the long perfect stride but there are not a lot of them out there."*

Gordie Clark agrees with Gorton and believes the prospects in the middle of the pack are the most difficult to judge.

> *"Skating is one of the hardest qualities to scout for any staff that I have been with. There is always an inconsistency of what an individual scout is looking at. What a scout sees as the top-end skater is easy, and the knock-kneed skater is easy, too, but it is the prospects in between that probably most of our NHL is made up of."*

So what do the scouts look at when they are trying to determine if these middle-of-the-road skaters will be able to make it in the NHL? Are there aspects within skating that scouts know are more important to the success of a player at the NHL level?

THE BIG PICTURE

How scouts approach the challenge of evaluating a player's skating varies, as *Scott Bradley* points out. Some break down the individual mechanics of a skater's technique, while others focus on a player's overall skating ability.

"The other scouts might look at edges or how he goes laterally. It's really a tough thing to project how much a prospect will improve his skating. There are so many parts of the stride you need to look at, even if you don't have a doctorate in skating. I have sat down with people that have broken skating right down, but I look at it as a whole. We all do it differently."

Tim Burke also likes to focus on the big picture. His main focus is on the race for loose pucks; he wants to see a prospect who consistently makes it to the puck before his opponents.

Scouts who look at the big picture, including *Gordie Clark*, like to use comparisons to get a sense of how a prospect would fit into the NHL.

"I think the biggest thing when you talk to most scouts is, 'Well, he reminds me of this guy or he reminds me of a Paul Coffey.' A lot of guys from different scouting staffs use that."

Marty Stein finds it useful to compare skating abilities during training camps and prospect tournaments, when prospects are matched up against current professionals. By noticing what areas the prospects struggle in against professionals, the scouts have a greater chance of identifying the correct characteristics for success.

"When we are looking at some of the kids that come into the prospect tournament at Traverse City, they were pretty good skaters at the junior level, but it's a whole other level here, and they come in and have difficulty keeping up to the play with some of the veterans."

Even doing some research into the player's background can give some insight about the prospect's skating potential. This type of insight can help with some of the projection, and *Rick Dudley* uses it to reduce mistakes.

> *"But there are times when you go to the rink and you find players that you know are going to be fine NHL skaters. Sometimes you will see a 6-foot-5 guy who is 180 pounds, then you have to get a little more background. If you think you are going to draft him, you might go so far as to check—is his dad 6-foot-5 and 180 pounds at age 40? All those things come into play, and the more you know, the better chance you have of not making a mistake."*

Breaking Down the Mechanics and Physiology

So, while some scouts take a big picture approach, others like to break down the mechanics of a prospect's skating. Because the prospects are not physically mature, projecting this can be an arduous task.

> *"It is not easy because there are at least four different skating components: top-end speed, quickness, lateral mobility, and, when you are talking about a defenceman, range is important. Then you have to start breaking it down into the mechanics of the stride and physiological makeup of the athlete. Does he have the structure to become more powerful and thus a quicker athlete?"*
>
> Rick Dudley

When it comes to the mechanics of the prospect's stride, scouts try to figure out whether the stride can be improved.

Most scouts and fans can see the players who don't bend their knees or who are knock-kneed, but it's the other little aspects that are harder to figure out. When *Jay Heinbuck* is watching a player's stride, he's looking for a hint that the flaws aren't going to be an issue moving forward.

> *"I often try to look at the stride itself and the mechanics of it. Is it the type of stride that strength and practice can improve? Or is that stride always going to hinder him, with little window for improvement?"*

Marty Stein looks for how smooth the stride is and whether or not there are any hitches, because in some cases when the prospect adds strength it can compound problems.

> *"When we see a prospect skate in junior, he has to have a strong stride with and without the puck and we need to project him in a couple years. Then we take that strong stride and add the physical strength, as we want a player that can keep up to the play and not arrive after it is over."*

Foot Speed

In a game that prides itself on speed, sometimes the fastest player does not always have the advantage. The terminology most often used by scouts to describe a player in full flight is *foot speed*. Scouts determine whether one player is faster than another by sight or by using a series of timed tests in a controlled environment.

While straight ahead foot speed is coveted by many, artificially testing it is overrated in the eyes of *Craig Button*:

"If you are going to evaluate guys on straight-ahead skating over a long distance, it opens up a question, 'How many times in the course of an NHL game does a player wind up, start at one blue line, skate around the back of the net, and make an end-to-end rush?' Well, almost never, so why are people evaluating those things?"

He thinks it's more appropriate to assess this vital skill in specific game situations.

"Foot speed is important, but it's how a prospect uses that foot speed in game situations, like how a prospect uses his foot speed to gain an advantage over a defender or to close space on a defender and erase the guy from the play or to break into an opening to receive a pass."

For example, both Kris Draper and Pavel Datsyuk use foot speed in their roles, but each has a different style. The easiest way to judge their abilities is to watch them in action.

"A perfect example would be Kris Draper versus Pavel Datsyuk. Draper looks much faster and is all over the place, but when the puck is on Datsyuk's stick, the game is much faster and he uses less energy. Now, a guy with a great head for the game can get away with less quickness and foot speed, but the guy with a limited head will eventually fall behind."

Craig Button

Jay Heinbuck also likes using peer-versus-peer action to judge foot speed and the player's ability to compete in the NHL.

"I am more concerned with the player's speed, and can that increase in terms of whether he can make the jump to the NHL level. How do you judge that on the ice? I try to look at that versus his peers. For example, did he just catch a guy on a back check? Did he catch the slow guy? Conversely, if the player I'm watching gets caught by a slow player, that does not bode well."

Marshall Johnston, Director of Professional Scouting, Carolina Hurricanes, observes four main parts of skating (quickness, foot speed, agility, and balance) but he suggests that foot speed is the one area that a prospect might be able to live without.

"If foot speed is the only liability, then you gamble that it can be improved. It's not going to keep him from playing, only limit his success."

But *Tim Burke* still likes to use it as a measure for lower-ranked players.

"When you go to the lower-skilled prospect, you may look for more foot speed and quickness because they must use their feet; they have a specific job that does not require them to make high-end plays with the puck."

Quickness

Most hockey fans know the difference between a player's quickness, which is his ability to get off the mark, and foot speed, which is his speed at full flight. However, scouts do not always agree about which skating attribute is more important.

Quickness certainly has value, and a player's quickness and his ability to use it effectively can make the difference between playing in the NHL or not.

Although a scout's profession is to see things that fans don't, even they can be mesmerized by flashy speed that accomplishes little. *Button* cites the 2003 NHL Draft as proof.

> *"If a scout was evaluating Corey Perry's ability to break open into an area around the net and beat people one-on-one, then the question I ask is, 'Why was he drafted 28th overall?' Somebody missed it. I don't care if you are in the NFL, the NBA, MLB, or the NHL, scouts get wowed by what I call flash skills. Players need to get open quickly in tight areas and use that ability effectively. Corey Perry always used that ability effectively in junior and that would translate to the NHL. In my opinion, people missed it because they are looking for the wrong things."*

Just as he does with foot speed, *Craig Button* uses a game-situation approach to evaluate quickness.

> *"So, you are looking at that two-step quickness, three-step quickness, and a scout is looking for those situations in a game. This is where a player has to beat another player one-on-one."*

When *Tony MacDonald* considers whether or not a prospect has enough quickness to change gears and create separation between himself and an opponent, he must remind himself that most prospects lack leg strength, which will come with maturity.

"Well, leg strength is a big issue with some prospects, and it inhibits the speed with some players. A scout has to take that into consideration. The kids that can show the balance and agility needed, but not always consistently, we know once they get strength they will have the good skating that can change gears."

MacDonald and his staff often use Erik Cole as a model for prospects they are considering. Cole is particularly known for his two- and three-step quickness, which allows him to change speed and break away from an opponent. When he was a college player, he was a good skater but he didn't always show that separation speed. When he matured physically, it became more consistent.

"One of the guys that we have on our roster and use as a model for skating is Erik Cole, as he has deceptive speed with the ability to change gears. When he comes down on defencemen, they usually underestimate how fast he is going until it's almost too late."

Agility and Lateral Movement

Assessing the subtle nuances of the agility and lateral movement of an underdeveloped skater is challenging for a scout. One thing *Doug Rose* will look for is how a prospect turns and moves in odd angles in tight spaces, in particular, the angle of his skates in those situations. Assessing whether a player does this consistently or just needs to be instructed properly is something talent evaluators keep in mind. Highly skilled skaters understand by altering the angles of their skates they can create time and space other than quickness and speed.

"Adjusting foot movement as it applies to creating a greater angle to the developing play so the puck carrier can exploit the defenders. It can decide the outcome of a game by learning to adjust your turn so you can go east-west as easily as north-south when you are attacking a defenceman off the rush to create separation to give the player enough time to take a shot on net."

SCOUTING SCORECARD

☐ Does the prospect have a long stride?
☐ Does he exhibit leg strength and power?
☐ Can he move laterally?
☐ Can he skate fast with the puck?
☐ Can he skate fast without the puck?
☐ Can his quickness create space?
☐ Does he bend his knees?
☐ Does he have good balance?

CHAPTER 9

Puck Skills and Puck Movement

"Some of the things we look for as scouts are good vision and offensive concepts—it's more than skate fast and shoot. You have to be able to think and see the ice, along with soft hands with a passing touch."

Tony MacDonald, Director of Amateur Scouting,
Carolina Hurricanes

Other than skating, puck-handling is the skill set that is most obvious to the general hockey fan. It's easy to pick out the NHL players who can dangle the puck or make laser-beam passes through traffic. The challenge for scouts is to pinpoint those skills in a 17-year-old player, dissect his positive and negative tendencies, and project his abilities to the NHL.

It can be difficult to separate the synergy of a player's hands, feet, and decision-making ability. However, it's important to do so because using technically perfect hands and wrists is the key to maximizing stickhandling and puck-moving skills.

I sat down with a group of scouts and hockey skills coach Doug Rose, who has worked with many NHL, AHL, WHL, and NCAA players, to discuss puck skills and puck movement. As they break down the different aspects of a player's puck skills, scouts attempt to determine not only the current level of ability, but also the player's overall potential.

Scott Bradley believes that skill with the puck is mostly a natural ability.

> *"Puck-handling and passing skill is almost an art in itself, and it's a skill that requires touch and feel with giving and receiving passes in tight traffic as well as in motion. It's a combination of many things, and either you have it or you don't. As coaching and experience steps in the player can improve it a little bit, but it is an art."*

HANDS, WRISTS, AND ARMS

When evaluating players' puck skills, some scouts look at the placement of the hands.

> *"A large part of evaluating a player's puck skills is how comfortable his hands are together on his stick. If the bottom hand is too low, it brings his whole upper torso forward."*

> Doug Rose

The placement of a player's hands on his stick seems like a small matter, but the effects of misplacement can be big, as *Rose* points out:

"The player does not get the same vision down the ice as he would get if his hands were higher. To compensate for that there also needs to be a little more knee bend as well. If the hands are a little higher on the stick, the player will get a much better idea of what is ahead and surrounding him."

When it comes to the importance of hand placement on a player's stick and how it affects his play, *Tony MacDonald* agrees with Rose and points to Patrick Kane as an example.

"You look at a kid like Patrick Kane. Back at his draft year he was considered a small player and still is, but the way he holds his hands fairly high on the stick means he is not a crouched-over skater. That enhances his ability to move the puck and his vision on the ice."

How a player rotates his wrists has an impact on how effectively he can stickhandle and pass the puck. Colton Gillies, a first-round draft pick of the Minnesota Wild, was instructed by Rose to alter how and where he holds his stick. Here *Rose* notes the importance of proper wrist action:

"I took Colton Gillies, who at the time was a first-round WHL Bantam draft pick, and he was holding his top hand wrong and locking his wrist. It is so critical not to have that top hand locked when you want to turn your stick since you

will end up turning your whole arm. If your wrist is relaxed and you move your hand up a little bit, your little finger is literally hanging on top of the stick by a thread and it's almost overtop of the knob of the stick. That way you can roll your wrists more effectively while keeping your elbow on that top hand down."

From a scouting perspective, *Rose* points out it's an easy thing to notice on a player, and it can drastically affect his offensive production.

"When players keep their top hand elbow too high, they become less effective in handling the puck. But when the player's elbow is low, it allows the puck carrier much quicker hands."

Jay Heinbuck doesn't look at hand placement as closely as he looks at arms. He thinks the natural motion of a prospect's arms as he delivers the puck gives scouts important clues about his abilities.

"Not so much where his hand placement is on his stick, but we will pay attention to what his arm movement is and how he is delivering that pass. Can he move it quickly with something on it and are the passes flat when they are required to be flat or are they wobbling? If he is making a saucer pass, can he get it over sticks and is it touching down flat on the ice on target? What does his arm delivery look like and does it come naturally to him, or does it look kind of rigid and forced?"

ON THE RUSH AND IN TRAFFIC

Many could assume that if players can handle the puck in traffic, they will have the same effectiveness on the rush. But *Rose* points out that those two on-ice situations should be handled differently.

> *"Many times a player will handle the puck too close to their body when on the rush, the same as they do in traffic. Because of this tendency, the puck basically becomes like an anchor and slows him down when he's trying to build momentum on a rush."*

While in traffic, it's important for a player to keep the puck close to his body to avoid turning it over, but when he's on a rush, this technique doesn't work because it slows him down and he'll have difficulty seeing opportunities. Although players are taught from the beginning to keep the puck in front of them and their heads up, doing this at speed and under duress is obviously difficult. *Rose* looks for players who can perform that skill under the most difficult of circumstances.

> *"The player must have the puck farther ahead of him so he is forced to look up ice and not at the puck. He will know where it is because he can feel it on his stick."*

Mario Lemieux is a perfect example of a player who kept his head up and was able to split the defencemen, throw the puck to an area past them, and skate to that area. Sidney Crosby and Zach Parise have also begun to send the puck to a hole and skate into it with more frequency and effectiveness.

It's important to keep the puck out in front when on the rush, not just because it's what scouts look for, but because it creates more opportunities for the player.

> *"There are advantages for a player getting it out in front of him, as it will not stunt his skating stride. It also gives the player more choices with puck movement, whether he passes, shoots, or holds and stickhandles."*
>
> Doug Rose

TIME AND SPACE

The evaluation process is made even more challenging because when players move to a higher level, the increased size and speed of the opposition causes a reduction of available time and space. Scouts must question whether or not a player can continue to make quick decisions and good plays under that kind of duress. Most scouts agree that at the junior level a prospect will have two seconds to make a play, in the AHL that is reduced to one second, and NHL players have only half a second.

Craig Button thinks that how a prospect manages the time and space he's given is important in the evaluation process.

> *"When you are trying to project players to the NHL level while they're still given a lot of time and space in junior or college, you are evaluating—can he make an NHL pass? I think in the NHL so much happens so quickly in such small spaces that it's not just the ability to make a pass but to do it instantly in a small space. So you are not watching how they pass the puck, but how quickly the prospect sees*

what is available to them and then their ability to make the pass."

Tim Burke agrees, and adds:

"More important is: can they make plays with the puck without time and space and stay in the play? Because some guys become that one-on-one all-puck-skill player and a scout knows that will not translate to the NHL. The reason for that is he does not use his linemates effectively."

Burke cites two prospects he previously scouted as examples:

"A great example would be when Chris Drury was in a high school game at an awful level and still found a way to get every player involved in the game. He did it by moving the puck quickly and precisely, and sometimes he never got it back. On the other hand, you can go back to Troy Mallette, who dominated bantam hockey with the puck and then never made the transition as a playmaker. It was because he never got accustomed to using his linemates on a consistent basis."

PUCK MOVEMENT

For *Rick Dudley*, it goes beyond just getting the puck to the right place; he points out that *how* the players get the puck to teammates is of equal importance. Many times we see players with the right intentions, but they just can't seem to deliver the puck to the exact spot. Players who can do both draw the attention of scouts according to *Dudley*.

"There are several different things, like soft hands, the suitable firmness of the pass in a given situation—will a prospect use a soft pass when he needs to and let a player skate into it? Or another time, if he has to get it past a couple of reaching sticks, does he puts a lot of zing on it?"

Harkie Singh focuses on whether or not the prospect can move the puck efficiently while he's in motion.

"The biggest thing for me is how these prospects' puck skills hold up when they are moving their feet with speed. If you look at a lot of players, even at the NHL level, they do not move the puck, receive the puck, or handle the puck at full speed. It's mostly done when stationary or done off a cycle or tight areas, and you almost never see players do that in open ice. If a player can skate with the puck and make plays at full speed at the junior level, that's a start. Since the game gets faster at the next level, I personally look for players that can do it consistently."

Like all scouts, *Singh* likes to look to the past for player comparisons.

"Remember the days when Mark Messier would shoot off the fly or come down the off wing? It's happening less and less over the years, although Alexander Ovechkin and Sidney Crosby still do it, but they are a dying breed."

Not just where a player passes the puck but how a player releases the puck from his stick can directly impact the effectiveness of his passing accuracy. The position of the puck in relation to his body or how he loads the puck before passing is a critical aspect of breaking down a player's passing ability according to *Doug Rose.*

"When making an efficient pass, first of all having a good feel for the puck on your (tape stick) and you want to be looking ahead and at your target. Whether you are skating or standing still, typically you will still load the puck from the left side if you are a left-handed shot and from the right side if you are a right-handed shot because if the puck is too far in front of the player they will just push the puck so a player does not want the puck too far in front of their body otherwise it is all arms."

Tony MacDonald looks at the resourcefulness of a player. The ability to handle the puck and make plays in less than ideal circumstances is a key attribute that he looks for. The players that can perform these feats tend to put less weight on their sticks and have greater fluidity of their upper body.

"If he can take a puck off the skate or a pass that is behind him and still control the puck without it bouncing off the stick, those are the things a scout is looking for in terms of puck movement."

Now, choosing the correct alternative and making a crisp pass is one thing, however, the key is to do it consistently. *Marty Stein* believes that successful puck management also requires the ability to handle pressure.

"The consistency is what we look for and does this player make the right pass or does he simply panic far too often? When he is in trouble, will he just bank it off the glass or throw the puck away?"

"There are different levels of puck poise depending on their league and development because a rookie will just panic if he sees only one option, like a quarterback in football when he doesn't see all the options in front of him. One of the biggest things we see in puck movement is the crispness of the pass and the patience the prospect has with the puck under duress. We're looking at if the kid can see all the passing choices he has and get the puck to the right spot."

Jeff Gorton draws comparisons to a couple of current NHL players when trying to dissect a prospect's capability to handle stress.

"Some of the players in the NHL have high assist totals, like Marc Savard or Joe Thornton. Both have the poise to hold on to the puck for what seems like seconds longer, but in reality it is a second, and allow the play to develop longer. It is like they play chess with the opponent, and these are the same things we look for in prospects."

PUCK SKILLS FOR DEFENCEMEN

Because of the way the NHL is being played now and how the rules are enforced, a prospective defenceman's poise with the puck is key. New rules prohibiting obstruction mean that they can't hold up forecheckers, so defencemen have less time to make decisions with the puck. Only a decade ago, a defenceman's skill at moving the puck was not considered as essential for some NHL organizations. Now, fast thinking and elite passing are valuable assets. The days of the lumbering, slow-footed blueliner who could bank it off the glass are quickly going the way of the dodo bird. The last few NHL Entry Drafts have proven the importance of these skills with the selection of defencemen such as Cam Fowler and Duncan Keith.

Tim Burke watches how quickly the puck moves off a defenceman's stick. Not only is the speed of the puck coming off the stick important to Burke, but he's also interested in whether or not the defenceman understands when to pass, stickhandle, or shoot the puck.

Rick Dudley looks for accuracy, but more importantly he wants to see the ability to maintain composure.

> *"More than anything I watch for accurate passing of the puck and how he finds a player while under duress, which is probably the most difficult thing to do. A lot of players can pass in a given situation without any pressure, but when they are pressured that is a whole different ball game—especially when you are talking about defencemen, it's everything."*

Gordie Clark references one of his own prospective defencemen who turned pro quickly and had puck-moving acumen.

> *"An example of a puck mover is a guy like Mike Del Zotto, who stands out even as a junior. Instantly you see that he is a prospect that could play in your top four one day. The*

whole game now for a defenceman is moving the puck, and they are not allowed to touch a forward or hook and hold. They must go stick to puck and read where to go, and you better have the feet to get your body in the right position since you can't put a stick on a guy."

SCOUTING SCORECARD

❑ Does the prospect place his hands high enough on the stick?

❑ Are his wrists relaxed?

❑ Does he use the appropriate level of firmness in his passes?

❑ Does he have a natural arm movement or is it stiff and forced?

❑ Can he adjust the type of pass he uses depending on the situation?

❑ Does he keep the puck close to his body in traffic?

❑ Does he allow the puck to move farther ahead when he's on the rush?

❑ Can he maintain control of the puck at high speeds?

❑ Does he use his teammates effectively?

❑ If he's a defender, can he move the puck out of danger quickly?

CHAPTER 10

Shooting the Puck

"You hear announcers say, 'Oh my god, he picked the corner,' then you see the replay and there is no way he saw it as he didn't even look up. But he knew where the net was and where the goalie was in relation to the net."

Gordie Clark, Director of Player Personnel,
New York Rangers

There are countless different shots and all are dangerous; however, finding a natural goal scorer is like hitting the jackpot for scouts. The importance of the potential result means that scouts evaluate a player's shooting ability with a great deal of anticipation. In particular, they watch for the subtleties that make the difference between a 40-goal scorer and a 20-goal scorer.

BODY POSITION

Gordie Clark looks for players who understand the impact that different body positions can have when they're in the slot, including giving them the best angle to the net. How the play develops will dictate where a player should position his body in relation to the net and the defending forwards and defencemen. However, finding a prospect who recognizes the importance of proper positioning in the slot can be rare.

> *"There are a lot of guys that can hammer a puck, but that doesn't necessarily mean they can score with the puck. I know when I was coaching Cam Neely in Boston I had to do a lot of the video research and watch the power plays. I had to watch Brett Hull a lot, and the biggest thing that stood out for me with him and other goal scorers is they know how to play the slot. I find too many prospects who are standing still in the slot waving the stick in the air saying, 'Here I am, here I am,' and there are two defenders between them and the centre, who is going around the net or into the corner."*

Clark notes that it's important for players not only to be aware of body position but also to have the maturity and good sense to be able to adjust it as needed.

> *"You would then watch Neely and Hull, and they would move a little left or a little right to be able to present their stick to the passer, whether it was Adam Oates or Craig Janney it didn't matter. It might put their angle off a little bit on the shot and they are not right in the middle slot, but they move over a little bit so the passer can get it to them."*

A QUICK SHOOTING RELEASE

Another key to becoming a great shooter is having a quick release. Scouts almost universally believe that a prospect with a quick release on his shot has a better chance of scoring at the next level. Although a quick release is stressed in the NHL, with the improvement in shot blocking and an increasing number of sticks in the lanes, it's becoming more important at junior level, too. *Jeff Gorton* points to Phil Kessel as an example of someone with a naturally quick release.

> *"The number one thing that jumps out at me is the release when you look at a guy like Phil Kessel in his draft year. When he was younger, his release caught your eye right away. How does a guy get the puck off his stick that quick in traffic with a defender all over him? Those are the type of players, like Brett Hull who did not have the puck on his stick very long, that will score consistently."*

It's important to remember that prospects have more time to make a play in junior hockey than they will in the NHL. *Gordie Clark* also stresses the value of getting the puck on net quickly rather than taking the time to see exactly where you're shooting.

> *"Obviously there are a lot of times when Hull and Neely had a guy in their face or rushing them when they got the puck. The main thing these guys did was they knew where the 6x4 was and they got their shot on the net. These shots were not from particularly far out and with all the big bodies around they didn't have time to take a look. They*

knew where the net was and where the goalie was, and the biggest thing they did was getting the puck on net. A lot of other players would shoot wide."

Marty Stein has noticed a lack of shooting at the junior level and has no time for prospects who waste opportunities while on the power play.

"The release and the accuracy are the most important things for a prospect's shot. Especially as the players, even juniors, are bigger and they are taught how to get into shooting lanes and block shots. It drives me crazy when you see a power play at the junior level and these players are moving the puck around and moving the puck around. In the end, they maybe get two shots off on the power play and waste a bunch of time. If a prospect can get the shot off quicker, it makes the goaltender work, and the more shots at the net, the better chance they have to score. They will not catch grief from us for shooting the puck."

As a former goaltender, *Scott Bradley* likes watching shooters in the warm-up to get a good idea of their efficiency.

"You look at release and quickness along with heaviness of a shot, and scouts tend to gravitate towards prospects that are consistently scoring. I like to watch a prospect shoot in warm-up. I was a goalie, so maybe I have a little bit better feel for the heaviness and the quickness of a shot. Not saying the shooters that are scouting are different, but we all have to watch his quickness and if he is picking for corners."

SHOOTING ACCURACY vs. POWER

When it comes to the question of which is more important, the power or the accuracy of a shot, *Tim Burke* points to Dany Heatley and Ilya Kovalchuk. Both players are examples that a prospect does not have to shoot hard to score.

> *"Number one is not missing the net. I think with a lot of these scorers, like the Heatleys and the Kovalchuks, they don't miss the net that often. Most pucks cross the goal line at 65 miles per hour, so there ends the myth about the hard shot. How hard the shot is isn't as important as the puck on the tape and off the tape and on the net, not trying to find holes."*

Marshall Johnston believes that accuracy is the biggest difference between average and great goal scorers.

> *"The biggest difference in goal scorers is from continually missing the net to getting shot after shot on net (Mike Bossy never missed net—including in warm-ups)."*

Wayne Gretzky, who is the NHL's all-time leading goal scorer, didn't blast pucks past goaltenders. His quick shots kept the goalies off balance and didn't give them time to set up; this was the hallmark of his goal-scoring prowess.

> *"An example is a guy like Wayne Gretzky, who did not have an overpowering shot. He always put the puck on net quickly and in the right spot where the goalie couldn't get at it or couldn't put himself in a position to make a save."*
>
> Tony MacDonald

Players with short follow-throughs will often have more accurate shots. *Tim Burke* notes that two NHL scoring legends, Mike Bossy and Guy Lafleur, both had short follow-throughs.

> *"Mike Bossy and Guy Lafleur talked about putting the puck on net and making the goalie make a save even if they couldn't see the net. I look for a short but firm follow-through where the prospect is guaranteed better accuracy. When you have a longer follow-through and a sweeping motion, the puck will get deflected a lot by defenders."*

Accuracy is particularly important when defencemen are shooting the puck. *Tony MacDonald* thinks a couple of brothers from the Czech Republic both had a knack for getting the puck on net.

> *"Shooting the puck hard is not the most important thing, especially with defencemen. The defenceman that can get the puck on net and on target is pretty important. I would have to say Tomas Kaberle is one of the better ones who is efficient at that. His older brother, Frantisek, was the same way when he won a Stanley Cup with us here in Carolina."*

He points out that a defenceman's accuracy is even more important on the power play.

> *"A good power play guy is not good because he overpowered anybody with his shot but because he got the shot through, so you always have a chance for deflections and rebounds.*

I think that is an underrated part of it and it's something scouts look for."

DECEPTION

When scouts are looking at goal scorers, they often look for the ability to deceive the goaltender. *Harkie Singh* likes to see if the prospect keeps his feet moving when he shoots and tries to use some trickery to gain an advantage on the goaltenders.

> *"When I look at a player shooting the puck, I like to see if they use the opportunity in front of them. Like when Sakic used the defenceman as a screen and quickly wrist shot the puck through his legs instead trying to beat the defenceman one-on-one. I like to see a prospect continue to move his feet while he shoots and hide the puck with a little stickhandle right before the shot. This is so he isn't telegraphing his shot and is using some deception."*

Jeff Gorton agrees that deception is key and likes to watch the goaltender for clues about how effective the deception was.

> *"It always opens your eyes when a prospect scores goals, but a scout has to look at how he scores goals. Is it his quick release, is he unbelievably accurate, does he have deception? You are looking at all those things. Generally, the goalie will tell you, and a scout can learn a lot from the goalie's response after the shot. For example, if the goalie looks back, the shooter probably used some type of deception, like he was going to go another way and he changed at the last second."*

HAND PLACEMENT WHEN SHOOTING

A relaxed grip gives a player more hand and wrist flexibility. *Harkie Singh* keeps track of where a player holds his hands when he shoots and notes if he can make the adjustments necessary to get the shot away.

> *"A player must adjust his hands, as sometimes he will get a pass that is not at his feet or aligned properly. It's important to see how a prospect holds his stick, as sometimes they hold too tight. You have to be able to move your hands smoothly, for example, when a player is trying to tip a puck and it's three feet in the air and he's batting for pucks. Back in the day, Wayne Gretzky used to bank pucks off goalies and defence-men by changing where his hands were on his stick."*

Jay Heinbuck really notices hand placement when the player goes to the backhand.

> *"When it comes to hand placement on a player's stick, it becomes more prevalent on a backhand shot. The player has to drop his bottom hand to get any kind of velocity—more than on a forehand shot, because you can snap your wrists quickly. The ones that don't get the velocity on their back-hands tend to have their hands higher and closer together, like they're in stickhandling mode."*

THE NATURAL SCORER vs. THE DEVELOPING SCORER

Obviously natural goal scorers are ideal for NHL teams, par-ticularly because, while a potential player can sometimes surprise you, it's unlikely that a prospect who doesn't score consistently at the age of 18 will develop into an NHL scorer. That being said, *Jay Heinbuck* cautions that scouts have to watch carefully so they don't miss out on a potential goal scorer, because sometimes a player's flaw is fixable.

> *"For example, sometimes when a kid takes a slapshot he doesn't seem to take any ice. We were all taught that when you take a slapshot you are supposed to hit the ice behind the puck to create some flexion in your stick for velocity. You see some guys where they are hitting the puck without hitting the ice, consequently they don't have a hard shot. Now can that be corrected or is that going to be a tough habit to break?"*

The players who are more likely to develop once they reach the NHL are European players, who blossom once they come to understand the North American style of play. The traditional European mentality is to pass first and shoot second, and sometimes it's hard to alter that in a player. This isn't the case with every prospect, but it's something that plays into decisions of scouts. *Gordie Clark* notes one prospect who didn't have a big goal total as a junior but turned into a dangerous scorer in the NHL:

> *"There are not a lot of guys for me that turn into great goal scorers if they haven't been that at a lower level. But Gaborik at 17 was one. I was looking at both Gaborik and Dany Heatley when I was working for the Islanders. We were going to be picking high in the first round, and Gaborik got so many breakaways because he was so bloody*

fast, but he was not finishing them off. … Now Gaborik has turned out to be a better goal scorer once he learned to take the shot. He could get breakaway after breakaway in Europe, but he was not going to get away with that here, and so he developed a shot from the outside."

SCOUTING SCORECARD

❑ Does the prospect have the correct body position?

❑ Is he willing to take the shot, even if he can't see the net?

❑ Is his shot accurate?

❑ Is he able to quickly release the puck from his stick?

❑ Does he have a short, firm follow-through?

❑ Is he able to fool the goaltender?

❑ Does he have a relaxed grip on his stick?

❑ Is he a natural or will we have to invest in teaching him to shoot?

CHAPTER 11

Physical Game

"When it comes to aggressiveness and physicality, it's about work ethic, composure, knowing when to be aggressive in certain situations, competitiveness, and how a prospect takes charge. It's interesting because not every player has the ability, and I think it comes down to his character and work ethic."

Scott Bradley, Director of Player Personnel, Boston Bruins

You'd think that physical game, such as bodychecking, winning one-on-one battles, or fighting, would be easy enough to scout, as it should be an obvious feature to pick out in a player. However, as with other skills, there's always more to it than meets the eye. Scouts need to determine whether a player has the moxie to disregard his well-being in the interest of making the play. Prospects must also show a certain level of competitiveness and commitment.

A player who is consistently willing to be aggressive and physical benefits his team not just immediately after impact, but also by developing a reputation as a disruptive player. *Rick Dudley* points to Darcy Tucker as an example:

"You look at Darcy Tucker and he wasn't a great skater, but he certainly had the willingness, good timing, and he was going to arrive in a bad mood. The thing you notice with a player like that is the defencemen move the puck a little quicker than they want to when he's around. Instead of the defenceman making the best option in a pass, maybe he's thinking any choice is good so long as it moves the puck before a guy like Tucker or Ben Eager arrives."

ATTITUDE

The word that comes up consistently when scouts discuss a physical player is not size or strength, but willingness. *Craig Button* certainly believes that willingness is key.

"I always say, 'Will is a skill,' so it's the will to do the things necessary to win the game."

Rick Dudley agrees willingness is a key to playing an aggressive type of game, but he feels that there are additional skills required to be an effective physical player.

"There's no question that willingness is one of the biggest parts of playing that style of game. But also, skating and timing come into it, and timing is not easy to teach. You can tell by watching a player enough times that he consistently

makes enough contact that he could probably do that in the NHL."

Button cautions against forgetting to account for a player's physical maturity and style of play when assessing their physical play. He uses a former first-round draft pick who is currently playing in the NHL as an example:

"Scouts said, 'Look at him, he won't go in there and take the hit.' I remember saying to scouts that I was working with, 'He's 160 pounds and has no chance to knock that guy off the puck. So why do you want him to go in there and bang his head against the wall and have no success? Wouldn't it be better to use his quickness to strip the guy of the puck?' I told the prospect, 'Why would you bother to do that anyway since you have no chance of success, so why not use your quickness?'"

While it's true that some kids don't have the current body mass to deliver a crushing hit, many are still able to take good angles and demonstrate that they understand timing. *Jay Heinbuck* likes to see a prospect who uses those skills and at least makes an effort to get his nose dirty once in a while.

"Is he at least going into traffic to get hit and bumped around and pay the price, or is he willing to get in on the forecheck? Will he try to make at least some contact, even if it's not hard contact? Is he there trying to disrupt the flow of the game? But if he plays on the perimeter, staying away from all contact, then that is a red flag."

For *Marty Stein* it comes down to the competitive nature of the prospect, regardless of whether or not he currently has the size. The Red Wings can point to defenceman Niklas Kronwall, who was about 5-foot-10 and 170 pounds when he was drafted. Despite his size, no one in hockey would dispute that he's a strong physical player, mostly because of his competitive nature.

> *"The bottom line is their compete level. There are a lot of bigger guys that are going to go in and battle and should win over the smaller players. At times, the bigger player has a tendency to take himself out of the play trying to make a big hit. When it comes to the smaller player, his level has to be really high because he's always going against bigger, stronger players. They have to be able to take a hit to get a puck out or to make a play."*

GIVING AND TAKING HITS

Once scouts get past the prospect's willingness, competitive level, and current physical maturity, the next step is to find out if he knows how to hit. How does a prospect line up to make contact with another player? Does he hit the correct part of the body to neutralize that player from the developing play?

There's a long-held myth that the physical players are just dumb Neanderthals, but that's no longer the case. To be successful in today's NHL, tough players must be smart as well. *Tony MacDonald* knows that a smart player is a more effective tough player. He points to Scott Walker, who suited up for his Hurricanes, as a perfect example:

"I use the example of Scott Walker, who played for Carolina and showed the battle level, courage, and willingness to get into those dirty areas. But he was smart about it and made his job a lot easier by reading the play and attacking it properly."

When evaluating bodychecking, *Tim Burke* doesn't want to see a prospect who just throws his body at the opposition. What Burke and other scouts want is a prospect who understands the value of hitting the midpoint of the body and can change his body position to ensure that's where he makes contact.

"If you're judging whether a prospect is a good bodychecker, more important than size is whether he hits the midpoint of the other player's body. When they neutralize the midpoint of the body when they check, they stop the play."

This ability to deliver a smart bodycheck in the right game situation is more effective than simply going out and trying to intimidate the other players. *Jeff Gorton* tries to determine if a prospect understands this or if it's something that will have to be worked on later.

"When a scout is looking at any player, he wants to know: is he willing to go out and finish his checks or is it something he does once in a while? We are looking to see if he gets all the body or does he miss and hit all glass? Effective bodychecking needs skill in willingness and timing. Just because a young prospect can lay a big hit, doesn't mean it's effective—does he expose his other teammates by putting himself out of the play when he is needed?"

Many believe that the ability to take a hit can impact the outcome of a game, and scouts put great stock in a player who's willing to take a hit to make a play. Players who aren't willing to take a hit not only risk causing a goal against their team but also send a message of passiveness. Keeping plays alive by using your stick and body to take a hit is a quality all scouts covet, especially *Tim Burke*.

"Receiving a hit is much more important than giving hits, because receiving hits and rubs keeps plays alive. Not a lot of guys get stick wins, but Wayne Gretzky would, and guys like Forsberg would get stick wins and body wins. The physicality, the impact hit, where they are in the rink, and who they are against is all important. Will this prospect finish off a Henrik Zetterberg hard or will he kind of lay off him because he thinks he is going to get beat?"

This ability to take a hit to make a play is a vital factor for *Harkie Singh* when deciding which prospect to draft or sign. He agrees with Tim Burke about the value of taking the hit and thinks that sometimes prospects don't understand the importance it has in the outcome of a game. Failure to take a hit can give a psychological boost to the opposing team, something *Singh* closely monitors.

"What we like to see is if a prospect can take a hit to make a play. That player may not be on the score sheet, but it could be a deciding reason in a goal. Or on the other side, if they don't finish their check because the player thinks it's not a big deal to let him go, it could end up being a

part of a goal scored against. Also, the player that does consistently finish his checks recognizes the psychological effect it has on the opposition. It may force the opposition to make decisions faster, resulting in a mistake, and the players that understand that are valuable."

When *Jay Heinbuck* is watching a highly skilled prospect, he gives them a little leeway if they avoid some body contact. However, he does note that if there is no willingness to do either the hitting or receiving, then the prospect probably has no future in the NHL.

"Sometimes you see guys that don't ever want to be in a position to get hit and that is a red flag. If he's an offensive player, I am not so worried, as there are some players that are so good with the puck that they aren't out there hitting. But conversely, they must be willing to take a hit to make a play. We are never exactly sure when players get bigger and stronger how effective they will be when they hit. But what I do know is if a prospect is not willing, then he will never be effective either way."

BOARD PLAY

Without a doubt, the area that receives the least amount of praise within the world of hockey is a player's effectiveness along the boards. Out at the rink, *Jeff Gorton* believes it's an underrated skill that scouts should want in a prospect, and he makes a point of watching it closely. He says that this skill set is vitally important for any organization whose philosophy is based on puck possession.

"Holding the puck and playing along the boards is a much-underrated skill, especially if you are trying to build a puck possession type team. If you see a guy that can play off the boards and absorb hits, not get neutralized, and then spin off the defender, that is something scouts definitely look for. If they can control the puck and wear down defenders, those are the qualities scouts want."

The Sedin twins were particularly good board players. *Scott Bradley* notes that once they got stronger their technique improved. The cycle game is physically demanding, and as the twins matured they became even more effective.

"You are not looking at his feet per se, and the Sedins dominated that area even when they were at the Under-18s and they were drafted 2 and 3 overall. They always had that skill and, over the course of time, they have gotten stronger. Maybe some scouts will look at how a prospect pivots out of a corner and how they point their toes, but I don't think that comes into it."

When *Rick Dudley* is watching prospects' board play, the first thing he notices are the kids who want to take the pounding. The players know that they're exposed, and he watches to see if they're going to set aside their fears and suck it up for the team.

"Certainly the willingness to play needs to be there and there are a lot of players that don't want to shield the puck because that means they are automatically going to be banged."

However, *Dudley* believes puck protection can be instilled in the players. A point of contention for him is that some coaches don't teach board play well, or at all, and the scouts end up putting the blame on the prospect.

> *"The one thing I discovered is that protecting the puck can be taught. The difference between one player and another is he has been taught properly, and something that is lacking in our game is the teaching aspect. I don't think the wall game is taught nearly enough. If you are an old coach like me, you can come away from the game and say, 'I'm not sure about the player, but I'm damn sure about the coach.' And a lot of it comes from the player's ability to play off the cycle."*

Dudley thinks Craig Ramsay does a great job of teaching board play. He feels the work he did with Fredrik Modin made all the difference in his game.

> *"The best example is Craig Ramsay, when he coached in Tampa Bay, who took Fredrik Modin. Freddie was a big, talented guy, but he was not a great puck protector until he met Craig Ramsay, and he taught him to protect the puck. Then Freddie became an All-Star."*

FIGHTING

Being able to effectively project a prospect's pugilistic abilities can be more challenging than one would think. This is something *Marshall Johnston* and most scouts contend with every time they watch prospects fight. How many times have we seen players come from the college or European leagues where fighting is not the norm and then go on to become solid fighters in the NHL? The opposite can also happen, particularly with junior prospects who were significantly more physically developed than their counterparts. So how does a scout evaluate if a player has the ability to fight effectively at the NHL level?

> *"One way that helps is by watching the opponents' reactions and is that successful? Plus, is it natural and does the player enjoy it?"*

Craig Button cautions that scouts can get into a bad habit of losing sight of the big picture, and saying to themselves, "This prospect should be able to do this and if he can't, he's no good."

> *"I must say we can get caught evaluating the wrong things. It's like in football—nobody asks an offensive lineman to return kickoffs, and they don't ask kick returners to play the wedge on the kickoff coverage, so why as scouts do we evaluate prospects based on things that are not their skills? It happens all the time!"*

SCOUTING SCORECARD

❑ Does the prospect show a willingness to take/deliver a hit?
❑ Does he know how to properly time his hits?

❑ Does he know how to line up to make effective contact?

❑ Does he consistently hit the midpoint of the body?

❑ Is he effective at battling for the puck along the boards?

❑ Is he a willing fighter and will he stick up for his teammates?

CHAPTER 12

Defensive Hockey

"How does a scout decide if a prospect has the ability to be an effective defensive player? Well, technique is teachable, but only if the 'willingness to pay the price' is there."

Marshall Johnston, Director of Professional Scouting,

Carolina Hurricanes

Playing without the puck is the most contentious issue a coach has with his players, especially when they are learning the craft. Considering that a player is without the puck for the majority of the game, one would think playing away from the puck would be his most developed skill. However, this is not the case for most young prospects. Many of them need a lot of work to understand the nuances of the defensive game, which requires work ethic, consistency, and sacrifice. Defensive tactics are taught later in minor hockey, after the kids have mastered the basics of skating, puck-handling, and shooting, which contributes to the lack of prowess. Unfortunately for the coaches, the success of playing good defence is rarely given the credit it deserves, and all the accolades tend to go to the players with offensive statistics.

Prospects find it easy to make the choice between the glory of being a point producer or being responsible defensively. However, the success of a team relies on good defence from every player—including the forwards. So scouts do focus on prospects who show good habits in the defensive zone and try to project whether or not they will be able to multi-task all the situations at the speed and tempo of the NHL. Many NHL hockey operations departments believe that so long as a prospect has good hockey sense and skating ability, any deficiencies in his defensive play can be cured through coaching. Depending on their team's priority, scouts may also look for players with good balance and lateral movement, enough speed to be able to challenge the guy with the puck, plus the ability to read plays, to be in the right place, and to cut off the ice on an approaching player. Scouts assess the defensive abilities of forwards and defenders differently; however, two attributes are required for both positions: hockey sense and a strong work ethic.

When evaluating prospects defensively, *Craig Button* reminds himself that skilled players always have the puck and defence is teachable. The key to the second part is the strong work ethic, as prospects may have the hockey sense but they also need the drive to succeed.

"Number one, so few prospects understand which angles to take or where to stand to position themselves. That is why

coaching and development is so important for prospects. When a prospect has the puck all the time, is physically dominant, and their skills are better, they never worry about things like gap control, taking good angles, and body position. That's because they can make up for those mistakes, but at the NHL level they can't. Number two, the prospect must be willing to work without the puck and show a determination to work without the puck, and certainly the player has to have awareness."

He also thinks scouts must do background work to find out the work ethic and determination level of prospects—are they willing to pay the price to learn and be coached? It sounds simple enough, however, some prospects aren't open to doing things a different way.

"You don't know, and it comes down to the prospect's willingness to be taught and learn, and a lot of background work goes into that. How coachable is the player and does he understand these are important to the game and does he want to improve in certain elements of the game?"

Button inherited his belief that defensive play can be taught from his father, NHL Central Scouting founder Jack Button. He cites Mike Bossy as an example of a player who proves it.

"When Mike Bossy was going into the Draft, people were saying, 'He can't check and he can't do this.' It came down to the New York Islanders' pick, and Bill Torrey came over to my dad and asked, 'What do you think about Mike Bossy?' Dad said, 'He's an unbelievable player. I know his

family well and he played on a junior team that was not
very good. He has an unbelievable skill set and you have
nothing to worry about!' So Bill went back to Al Arbour and
said, 'We have a choice here, Al. We have a guy who could
score 50 goals in the NHL. Now, he doesn't check very well
and doesn't play defence at this time. We have this other
guy who doesn't have the high offensive skills, but he works
really hard and has pretty good defensive awareness.' Al
said, 'You give me the 50-goal scorer and I will teach him
how to play defence.' And the rest is history."

ON-ICE SKILLS

Rick Dudley agrees that defence is teachable, but thinks that
some basic elements are also necessary.

"It comes down to a combination of things, and teaching
the prospects. The feet are a large part of it, and hockey
sense in general . . . and he does not necessarily have to have
it when he plays amateur. What he needs is the capacity
to read plays and to move quickly enough to be able to
challenge the puck carrier, and it's a combination of those
things."

When looking for good defensive players, *Dudley* uses a
few comparisons.

"I think Kris Draper is a perfect example, and I don't want
to say they have to have great feet, but he does everything
well. Also, when you watch Nick Lidstrom, he never seems
like he is in a position where he has to scramble too much

to eliminate a player who is trying to beat him. I played with Craig Ramsay for many years, and Craig was a guy that used angles, anticipation, and a great stick. He used those things to be an effective player. In terms of cutting off the ice on a player and being in the right place, Craig was tough to beat."

Tim Burke thinks that projecting the defensive potential of a prospect comes down to two feet. No, not the smelly appendages at the bottom of your legs, but the two-foot diameter around a player. What a prospect does within those two feet can give scouts clues about whether he can process information quickly and be proactive.

"I think in judging prospects' potential at the defensive game it comes down to two feet. Many of the junior players are two feet out of the play, when they are on the weak side especially, and they are not necessarily cheating. But we are looking for a player that knows where the puck is going and limits choices by using his stick and positioning first, not just chasing and craziness."

Correct body position is also important to *Burke*. Having good body position is a combination of many things and it varies depending on the situation. However, anytime a defender can use his body to restrict the time, space, and opportunity of an offensive player, he is demonstrating good body position.

"So for reference, when you watch a good defensive NHL player he always seems to be in the right place with his stick

and body. He will not allow the puck carrier to even make a play. Similar to when a goalie is in great position and the shooter does not take the shot, we give the goalie credit for making the play without taking a shot. Good defensive body position can nullify playmaking and nobody really sees that."

Burke thinks Nick Lidstrom is an excellent role model for scouts to use in evaluating body position and for coaches to use as a model to teach young prospects.

"Like when Nick Lidstrom plays his dots and he has his stick in position and the forward will turn away. He will not even bother to penetrate the zone and Lidstrom hasn't done anything the fans see. But another guy will chase on the wrong side of the puck carrier and it turns into a scoring chance."

When it comes to scouting the defensive attributes in a prospect, *Tony MacDonald* believes an important trait is whether or not the player consistently stays on the right side of the puck. Even if the prospect doesn't do anything else well defensively, being on the right side of the puck is a foundation that can be built from.

"One of the key things is the prospects that are consistently on the right side of the puck. If they are always on the right side of the puck, they are in a position to, if nothing else, at least angle and contain their check. Being on the right side of the puck allows the prospect to get proper body position and control that player better."

There are certain secondary abilities that *MacDonald* also favours when grading a prospect's potential to play a two-way defensive game. He targets the prospects that give out extra effort and realize that constant movement is essential.

"The prospects that have the competitiveness, second effort, and that keep their feet moving can be taught to be effective in the other areas of the defensive game."

Harkie Singh agrees with MacDonald and Burke regarding body position, but he also stresses that the ability to anticipate the developing plays is vital. *Singh* particularly looks at the prospect's ability to keep his head up and at his defensive play in the neutral zone.

"One of the biggest concerns for me is: how do they position themselves and how do they project what is going to happen three seconds ahead of the developing play? Do they keep their head on a swivel and try to angle players properly, especially in the neutral zone? Because I think that is where the game is won and lost."

The skills that are important to *Jay Heinbuck* differ slightly, depending on whether he is breaking down the defensive play of forwards or defencemen. For forwards, he focuses on prospects who are taking good angles to the puck carrier and not giving time and space to opposing players.

"With forwards it's important to take the proper angles. For an example, if they are forechecking with speed, they have to take the proper angle and take away options. Having said

*all that, I would not give too many demerits to a forward
for not doing that properly at this age—unless he looks like
he has no clue, then you have to question his hockey sense."*

For the blueliners, *Heinbuck* likes to see solid body position
and, if possible, the ability to angle players properly. This does
not always happen with young defencemen, but they must at
least show that they have the necessary skating and footwork
skills.

*"You can usually see most of those things, depending on the
position of the player. With defencemen you can obviously
tell whether they are angling properly in the defensive
zone. For a defenceman it's more important, but again, if
everything else checks out with good footwork and skating,
the other stuff can be taught."*

FACE-OFFS

Although winning a face-off can contribute to success on both
sides of the ice, it is of primary importance in the defensive
zone. The ability to control the puck in the defensive zone
by winning face-offs reduces the opposition's scoring chances.
This is why scouts make a point of observing which prospects
can win face-offs consistently. The scouts also watch what the
players do if a face-off is lost and note if they understand their
defensive responsibilities. The scouts know that players who
have the potential to win face-offs and be defensively responsible after a face-off have a greater chance of playing in the NHL.

*"If you can find a prospect that is beyond years in
maturity, is good on face-offs, has defensive ability on the*

penalty kill, and the talent—it's a bonus. Now, it's great that a prospect is willing to do things that will make him a successful defensive player, like blocking shots, but he still has to have talent."

Jeff Gorton

"There are more face-offs in the neutral zone, so being able to tie up your man without getting a penalty is very important. After the face-off you want to see a prospect have his skates pointed in the right direction and his stick in the passing lanes. Those little things are what scouts look for, as those defensive habits by prospects can translate to the NHL. I believe what John Tortorella said is true, that in the defensive zone 'playing safe is death,' and being aggressive and forcing the puck carriers to make decisions faster than they want to is key."

Harkie Singh

COACHING

Another challenge for scouts is trying to figure out how much of a prospect's defensive acumen is his own awareness and how much is just good coaching. All scouts appreciate the fact a prospect is coachable and able to follow the system, however, coaches are savvy and can hide the warts of a player. It's important to determine whether a player has the hockey sense and willingness to pay the price, because disguising faults can only last so long.

Jeff Gorton makes note of which players are put into tough defensive situations by the coach. The coaches can be helpful tools for scouts, as they know the capabilities of young players in the defensive zone.

"When you are looking at young 18-year-old players, whether it's for the NHL Draft or later in free agency, scouts want guys the coach can rely on because it is a big part of the game and there is so much coaching with Xs and Os."

The ability to separate the player from the coaching system takes a little time according to *Gordie Clark*. He points out that it is important to not let the coach's decisions completely influence yours, particularly who he uses on specialty teams. Coaches will employ strategies to give them the best chance to win games, and they certainly can't be faulted for that. However, sometimes their decisions conflict with the scouts' desire to evaluate a player in a certain situation. Scouts must trust that the coaches are putting the players out, or not putting them out, in certain situations for a good reason. Maintaining open communication with coaches can help the scouts to understand their rationale and to decipher how much of a player's success is attributable to coaching and how much to the player's talent.

"After a period of time you get to know the prospect at major junior or wherever they are playing and how the coach is playing them. If a guy is consistently going out on the first power play and he is not scoring goals, you start wondering why is he out there. The same as if a defenceman is out there killing a penalty and they are being scored on. Well, he doesn't have the ability to think a man down and break up that play."

When it comes to scouting a prospect's defensive ability, *Marty Stein* says improved coaching has made it easier to distinguish who has the potential. He mentions that because of this, offensive players now have a greater chance to alter their game as they mature than the past generation did. *Stein* scouted Brent Gilchrist, who was a prolific offensive force in junior hockey and made a successful transition because of his smarts.

> *"The prospects now are taught to be better defensive players than in the past. You can take a good offensive player and make him a strong defensive player if he is smart. You take Brent Gilchrist, for example, one of the top scorers in the WHL when he played, and he developed into a top defensive player in the NHL."*

Jay Heinbuck agrees that good coaching is key, and NHL teams hope that the junior coaches have helped weed out the prospects who will not cut it in the professional ranks.

> *"With coaching and repetition at different levels, it is going to get pounded into them when it comes to good defensive posture."*

ACCEPTING ROLES

Since the majority of offensive prospects coming out of their respective junior leagues will not become top-line NHL players, scouts wants to know if they will accept being a role player. In the past we have seen top scorers from the junior or college ranks who did not translate their offensive output at the NHL level. Not every forward will develop into a top-two-line forward and not every defenceman will be a top-four defenceman. So will a player swallow his pride to a degree and adapt to a more defensive role on the bottom lines? Trying to figure out which prospects have both the willingness and the ability to develop into solid defensive players is a million-dollar question. Scouts who identify prospects who have the potential to contribute defensively at the NHL level consistently provide success for their franchises.

The difference between a draft pick becoming a successful NHL player or a career minor leaguer is often simply a matter of playing good defence. This is a situation that *Scott Bradley* has come across many times in his scouting career. He has observed that players who had a checking role in the lower levels rarely make it to the NHL, as they lack the skills to handle the tempo. For *Bradley*, it comes down to finding guys who just want to play and steering clear of players who do not see the big picture.

"Over the years I have been doing this, the game has changed slightly. But you will see offensive guys coming out of the CHL or college that have been offensive producers and thrust into a defensive role. You think, 'He was never a checker in junior or college,' but it's harder for a checker to be a checker at the next level because the skill set and ability to read plays is needed. I think it's a willingness to accept a role to be a defensive specialist. That comes down to hockey sense and some guys that score big points don't really care about checking."

Jeff Gorton agrees and points out that the scouts never quite know whether an offensive player will swallow his pride and develop into a defensive specialist, which can cause scouts grief when evaluating prospects.

> *"A scout still wants to know if maybe they can be a fallback guy or a third- or fourth-line player, so willingness is definitely important. If you are talking about a kid who is a defensive player at a young age, I think they have to have some offensive ability. If you look at some of the players in the NHL that are checkers, generally speaking when they were younger they were pretty prolific players."*

When *Jeff Gorton* speaks to prospects he uses Freddy Sjostrom, who was a first-round pick at the NHL Draft, as an example. He was exactly what scouts are looking for in an offensive prospect, in that he was willing to use whatever tools he had to play in the NHL. The players who remain mired in the AHL, still trying to outscore the All-Stars and unwilling to see the opportunity in becoming a defensive player, make *Gorton* shake his head.

> *"Take a guy like Freddy Sjostrom who obviously was a gifted skater, and he figured out he is not going to be a 40- or 50-goal guy. He is saying to himself, 'How am I going to stay in the league? I am going to use my speed to take good angles and be someone the coach can count on and have a nice 10-year career.' There are still a bunch of offensive guys from the junior days trying to beat out the Ovechkins and Gaboriks of the world for top-two-line status. They never figure it out that they could have a nice long career by being a responsible guy in their own end."*

SCOUTING SCORECARD

❑ Does the prospect have a strong work ethic?

❑ Is he willing to be coached?

❑ Does he show good habits when playing without the puck?

❑ Is he willing to pay the price physically to play well defensively?

❑ Does he understand the importance of becoming a defensive player?

CHAPTER 13

Goaltenders

"Goaltending is always changing and adapting, and over the last 20 years it has had more changes than the other positions."

Corey Hirsch, Goalie Scout, St. Louis Blues

Over the past decade or so, new training programs have made goaltenders look almost robotic in their mechanics and consistency. These training programs make projecting goaltenders far more difficult, as they can begin to look very similar. In fact, Garth Malarchuk, Amateur Scout, Toronto Maple Leafs, says that after a while he can even pinpoint which players have trained with which coach.

Scouts also find it challenging to scout goalies due to limited opportunities to view them in action. Often goalies in their NHL draft year aren't the number one goalie on their junior team. This means that scouts will sometimes only have one or two opportunities to see them in action. *Malarchuk* offers this example:

> *"You know, I think that sometimes it's doing your home-work and sometimes being lucky helps when seeing a goalie. I remember the year Steve Mason was drafted and he didn't play very much for London; we caught him, I think, once or twice. We had limited viewings on him as a staff, but we had great dealings with him. He got two shutouts and I think they were both 1-0 games on the road where he was just unbelievable. We would have liked to see him more, but that is how it goes sometimes in the business."*

Dissecting all the individual attributes and determining the strengths and weaknesses in young goalies is not an easy task. Once they've broken them down, a scout must put all those parts back together to see if the whole is more than the sum of its parts. Generally speaking, scouts look for excellent skating, solid crease mechanics, the ability to use both the glove and the blocker, stickhandling skills, good vision, and mental toughness.

SKATING

As fans, we generally focus on the exciting aspects of goaltend-ing: a flashy glove-hand save or an outstretched, improbable pad save. However, according to *Corey Hirsch*, former amateur scout and current goaltending coach with the St. Louis Blues, it all starts with the feet. It's often said, and with good reason, that the goalie must be the best skater on the team. Due to the speed of the game, the faster a goaltender moves the more likely he will be in a position to stop or play the puck. A slower moving goaltender puts greater stress on the defence, especially down low when they are trying to contain quicker forwards.

> *"This is a huge factor, and the better a skater they are, the better a goaltender they will be. The smooth transition from one movement to another without any clumsiness or awkwardness is a must. When you do find a strong skating goalie they are almost graceful."*

Hirsch notes that NHL organizations are always willing to work with prospects to improve the finer points of their skating technique, including push-offs and edges, but they must be pretty good skaters to begin with.

CREASE MECHANICS

Once they've ascertained that a prospect is a good skater, scouts next look at his crease mechanics (which can loosely be described as how effectively a goaltender moves from one position to another). Today, new levels of analysis and detail have made goaltending less artistic and more mechanical. Many will remember the days of the stand-up goalies who wore skinny pads and had to come up with unique and innovative ways to stop the puck. This isn't the case anymore. Looking back, *Garth Malarchuk* finds it almost comical how much trouble goalies used get in if they even thought of dropping down.

> *"I remember when I played we were told to stand up, we weren't allowed to go down—coaches used to give us shit*

*for going down. Now they're down every shot. You go watch
a practice with goalie coaches and the number of things
they are teaching the kids is impressive. I mean everything
is so detailed, but in the end, getting past that detail and
that technique is critical."*

One of the first things the scout will observe is a goalie's
stance and whether it gives him an athletic base to start from.
The proper stance is crucial, as the rest of a goaltender's game
will fall apart without a sound base. *Corey Hirsch* cites Roberto
Luongo as an NHLer with an ideal stance—wide and solid.
When scouting, *Hirsch* looks for simple things.

*"A scout looks to see if his stance is athletic, with his chest
out and a good bend in his knees (but not too much of a
knee bend so he's not looking too small in the net)."*

Once scouts have determined that the goalie has a good
stance, they tend to move on to the positioning and angles a
goalie takes on a developing play.

*"We look for crease positioning where they are not too
far out and not too deep, so somewhere around the top
of crease. That's probably the best place to be—from that
point what does the shooter have to look at?"*

Corey Hirsch

Goalie scouts also evaluate a prospect's ability to recover
after the initial save has been made. A key part of this
is rebound control to prevent the opposition from getting
another scoring opportunity. However, that's easier said than
done, even for elite netminders, so scouts must scrutinize
this skill closely. *Hirsch* looks for good positioning and a fast

reaction time, and uses Marty Brodeur as an example of a goalie who has amazing shot recovery.

> *"Knowing where a puck is going is vital because controlling every rebound is so difficult. So, being able to recover back into a compact frame in the right place is crucial. Secondly, they need flat-out quickness and the ability to scramble and make saves others can't."*

SCOUTING THE SAVE

Obviously, for fans the most important aspect of a goalie's job is making saves; if he can't make the saves, their favourite team is going to have a very difficult time bringing home the Stanley Cup. Scouts also focus a great deal of attention on a prospect's ability to stop the puck. Below are the four main things they examine.

The Five-Hole

Goals scored between a goalie's legs, an area known as the *five-hole*, are much talked about among scouts and fans alike. If a netminder squeezes his leg pads together in time, it's considered routine, but if he doesn't, then it's a catastrophe. A bad five-hole can end a scout's interest in a goalie as fast as it begins. What the scouts want to see is the speed at which the hole closes and a goalie who can stay compact while moving side to side.

The Paddle Down

Sometimes a goaltender will lay his stick across the ice to block shots down low and in tight, which is known as the *paddle down* technique. The paddle down save has merit, but according to *Corey Hirsch*, it should only be used in specific situations.

> *"You want to see the goalie only use the paddle down technique during wraparound attempts and situations really in tight. A scout does not want to see a goalie attempt this technique when the puck is farther than 10 feet away from the net since they'll be committing down low and exposing themselves up high. The decision to use it and how tight the goalie keeps his stick to the ice is very important."*

The Glove Hand

Perhaps the most spectacular and esthetically pleasing save a goaltender can make is with his glove hand. How a netminder uses his glove can be as unique as his personality. A characteristic that many scouts will look for when scoping out a lethal glove hand is how relaxed it is. The balance between holding the glove in the right place and being fluid in motion is a key indicator for scouts. In response to the strength of goalies' down-low play, shooters have begun aiming higher in the net. Therefore, Hirsch likes to see the glove positioned a little on the high side. He looks for a relaxed hand because too much rigidity can result in rebounds.

The Blocker Hand

Opposite the glove hand is the blocker hand, which tends to be underappreciated and can be the biggest flaw in a young goalie's game. *Hirsh* points out that scouts closely monitor how many goals are scored between the blocker and the body.

"Well, firstly you want to see a netminder be compact so there is not a big hole between the blocker and his body. That is very important because it's a spot where goaltenders can often be beaten."

Although fans are used to seeing goalies at all levels direct pucks with their blocker, scouts know it's not an easy task. The challenge lies in not giving up rebounds off the blocker and in directing the puck to the correct location, which ideally is in the corner.

STICKHANDLING

Some coaches used to consider passing and stickhandling acts punishable by death. However, now these skills are coveted in a goalie. Netminders like Chuck Rayner were considered renegades for wandering out of the crease to play the puck, but in today's game, it's much more commonplace. However, *Corey Hirsch* warns against overplaying the puck.

"When it comes to passing, overplaying the puck can be just as detrimental as not playing it very often. It's like when you want your defencemen to make smart, safe puck movement, not play the puck just because they can."

What the scouts are trying to find are goalies who have practised the skill of passing the puck and, more importantly, understand when to do it. *Garth Malarchuk* thinks that it comes down to a matter of hockey sense.

"Goalies can make subtle, short outlet passes to the defence-men to help them against the forecheck. The best passers in the game don't overplay it, they just make the simple

*puck movement and recognize the appropriate situation,
like making a pass and catching a line change to save their
teammates 10 to 15 feet."*

Many scouts agree that the best way for a goaltender to learn stickhandling is to use a regular stick. Once they've practised enough to become proficient with a player's stick, they can move on to learn how to do it using their larger goalie stick. The glove and blocker are cumbersome and lack the subtlety of players' gloves. There are two common styles of hand placement to try to overcome this: the glove hand over the top of the stick or the more traditional glove hand under the stick. Either method can be successful; choosing one comes down to which is more comfortable for the goalie and which he's had the most practice with.

What bothers many NHL scouts is that, for goaltenders, much of the art of passing the puck has been taken away. The addition of the trapezoid behind the net has restricted the opportunities for goalies to pass the puck. However, according to scouts it is still a valued skill in a goalie's arsenal and is scouted just the same.

Scouts also look at a goalie's ability to poke check, but many worry that it's a potential disaster waiting to happen. Although *Corey Hirsch* finds that the poke check leaves goalies exposed, he does admit that scouts appreciate it when it's done properly.

*"I was never a big fan of the poke check because I felt it left
you vulnerable, but if you look at some of the best shootout
goalies today, a lot of them are going to the poke check."*

The key to the poke check is patience. A goaltender must use it at the last possible moment, and it's a rare, valuable skill that must be practised. The goaltender must hide his intentions and not dip his blocker shoulder too early. Scouts will also watch how smoothly and quickly the goalie's hand slides down his stick while still maintaining control.

BREAKAWAYS

Scouts grade young goaltenders on their proficiency in breakaway situations. Most scouts, including Corey Hirsch, Garth Malarchuk, and Tim Bernhardt agree that patience is the first thing they look for. Now the obvious answer is: if the goalie is scored on, then he needs work, but it's not always that simple. Sometimes, at the lower levels, goalies can get lucky against inferior shooters. *Corey Hirsch* says that once the breakaway begins, there's a checklist scouts can follow that makes determining a goaltender's skill in the area easier.

> *"Get some momentum moving backwards so if the shooter dekes, the goaltender can get to the post really quickly. Then it's about making the player shoot around the goaltender instead of through him. We don't want to see anything go through the legs or arms, and we want goalies to force them to make a perfect shot."*

VISION

Other important traits that scouts look for in a potential goaltender are his vision and ability to track the puck. The term *tracking the puck* is relatively new and refers to the ability of a netminder to find the puck in traffic and to know where it's going. This skill can make or break a career.

"Goalies that can't track the puck will be goalies that get beat through screens and get caught looking too often instead of reacting."

Corey Hirsch

Garth Malarchuk agrees that the ability to visualize the developing play is important.

"I call it goalie sense. Reading the play is huge, but a lot of that is that instinctive stuff, too. It's that ability to read the play and react quickly enough to what's happening because there's not a lot of time."

Scouts watch how goalies handle traffic because it's a good barometer for their overall hockey sense. They like to see if the netminder can find the puck and determine where the puck is going simply by watching the positioning and movement of the other players. Remember the scene in *Star Wars* where Luke Skywalker used the Force to help him block the laser beam when his shield was covering his eyes? Goalies need to use the same kind of instinct.

MENTAL STATE

An aggressive nature can be a tremendous asset to a developing goalie, and scouts are eager to find prospects who possess it. Considering that most NHL shots ring in at close to 65 miles per hour, *Corey Hirsch* thinks confidence can be the secret ingredient that sets prospects apart from one another. Many scouts are impressed by a netminder who shows fearlessness without being reckless.

"For many goalies, this is the secret to their game. Scouts will look for the goaltenders that have the ability to hang in there and not get backed off by fear and who aren't getting scored on by being too deep in their net."

But assessing goaltenders' mental and emotional attributes is not easy. The main clue for most scouts is body language and whether they show any fear. Constant movement in the goalie's feet, some call this *happy feet*, is a little indication of a lack of confidence.

"Body language is probably the biggest key, you do not want to see a goalie that looks afraid, even though he might be. If he does present himself as nervous and scared, or confident for that matter, it will reflect upon his teammates. The goalie needs to show his teammates that he's not rattled. If the goalie's teammates think he's rattled, then they begin to play differently."

Corey Hirsch

"You can tell in the stands that you know this guy is in control. This guy does not look like he is panicking, absolutely the way he skates, the way he stops a puck, gives it back to the referee, gets back up, does some movements. You can tell if somebody is really nervous or somebody is in control and relaxed."

Al Jensen, NHL Central Scouting

For *Tim Bernhardt*, Director of Amateur Scouting, Dallas Stars, the mental strength is more important than any physical attribute. He thinks how a goaltender handles his emotions and remains focused is what separates the goalies who make the NHL from the ones who do not.

"Their mental makeup is definitely a huge, huge factor. Their mental approach, their ability to read and react, those are much more important, I think, than whether he has a good glove hand or blocker."

While scouts look for prospects who are composed, they can never be certain whether or not a young goaltender has the faculties to handle the stress. However, confidence does tend to improve as they mature, in part because they learn that at least some of it is an act. *Corey Hirsch* advises them to watch the best in the business as a template.

"You look at some of the best goaltenders in the NHL and a scout can't tell when they are nervous, so long as they're confident and stone-faced. That is a characteristic a scout looks for in a young prospect."

Perhaps the one ingredient that *Garth Malarchuk* covets more than any other is a goalie's competitive instinct. In his opinion, the ability to continue to remain mentally focused while battling to make every save makes all the difference.

"I still think the biggest thing for goaltenders is the compete level and the ability to win important games or to play well in important situations. I think that it's like when you look at your clutch pitchers in baseball, the ones that come up with the big games when you need them. But I also

*think there is a gift there, like some goaltenders are special
in that sense."*

He uses Bill Ranford, who went on to win a Stanley Cup
with the Edmonton Oilers, as an example of a player with
a great competitive spirit. He was the kind of player who
rose to the occasion because he competed in every situation,
regardless of whether or not he was on a winning team.

Another skill that may indicate NHL potential is a goalie's
on-ice communication with his teammates. A goalie who is
confident enough to communicate well with his team and to
lead them is a valuable asset.

*"It's easier to evaluate at the junior levels as the crowds
are smaller and the noise level is less. It's wise to get down
lower, close to the ice, so you can hear them clearly and see
if they are talking and controlling the play. It's important,
since the goaltender can be a lot like a quarterback and
help their teammates by directing the play."*

Garth Malarchuk

*"I like guys, goalies that communicate and I find that there
are a lot of goalies I don't hear verbally communicating at
that age. It is a vital component for a goaltender moving
forward."*

Al Jensen

PHYSICAL ATTRIBUTES

A goalie's physical attributes have become more of a pressing
issue for scouts as the goaltending equipment continues to be
reduced in size. In addition, goal scorers have become more

adept at putting the puck in the upper half of the net. As a result, in the very near future 95 percent of the goaltenders in the NHL will be at least six feet tall. The small netminder will soon be a thing of the past, regardless of how talented and quick he may happen to be. Now, that is not to say small goalies can't make the jump to the NHL, but scouts are not eager to draft them.

It's fair to say that goalies are under greater physical stress than their teammates since they are on the ice for the entire game. Therefore, the potential durability of a goaltender is of great importance. *Corey Hirsch* believes that the ability of prospects to play through minor injuries is a must in today's NHL. He points out that the larger goalies have an advantage in absorbing physical punishment. The susceptibility of the smaller goaltender to injury is a serious consideration for scouts.

"The ability to play through injury is an aspect that we look at, and it seems the bigger goaltenders tend to be more durable these days with the crease crashing. Although, as a scout you never want to completely rule out a smaller goalie with ability."

SCOUTING SCORECARD

❑ Is the prospect an above-average skater?

❑ Does he have an athletic stance?

❑ Does he understand how to position himself to cut down a shooter's angles?

- ❑ Is he able to recover quickly after a save and control rebounds?
- ❑ Does he have an aggressive nature and a competitive spirit?
- ❑ Does he have a relaxed glove hand?
- ❑ Can he use his blocker effectively and accurately?
- ❑ Is he able to read and anticipate plays?
- ❑ Can he stickhandle and pass efficiently?
- ❑ Is he a leader?

CHAPTER 14

Defencemen and Forwards

"When you are talking forwards versus defencemen, there are a lot of different aspects that are going into it. The biggest obstacle we have in scouting is projecting what this prospect's identity is going to be when he is at his very best."

Scott Luce, Director of Amateur Scouting, Florida Panthers

Both defenders and forwards need to be evaluated on their skating, puck skills, hockey sense, and so on (and we discuss these in other chapters). However, due to the specific skill sets required for each, the individual positions should be studied separately. A casual fan might assume that each position is equally challenging to scout, but most scouts agree that defence is tougher to project. The slight nuances involved in a defenceman's game can be so subtle that scouts must take great care in watching for certain habits. Why certain players make the adjustment to the next level when others with similar talent do not is the mystery scouts must solve. Since defencemen lack the insulation that forwards have when it comes to making a mistake, they are often under more pressure than forwards.

SCOUTING DEFENCEMEN

One of the challenges facing scouts when evaluating a defenceman is understanding how that player defends. Since there are many ways a blueliner can be successful in the NHL, the scouts must define the prospect's key attributes and determine if they can project at the pro level. Defencemen have a longer development cycle than forwards as they travel from the junior ranks through the minor pros. *Scott Luce* thinks this contributes to the difficulty of scouting defenders.

> *"When you are drafting defencemen you have to be a little cognizant of their development curve. What is he going to be and what is their position going to be with their amateur team, then their minor pro team, and then eventually the NHL team? Those are the things that make it very difficult—how you get past that."*

Skills

Jeff Gorton watches for a defenceman who can handle a high tempo pace while retrieving pucks.

"Well, right away you have to find out if the prospect can play at a certain pace, and if it's a defenceman, can he retrieve a puck quickly and quickly move it out of the zone? ... What separates really good players are those that can make those plays under constant pressure."

When he evaluates defencemen, *Rick Knickle*, Amateur Scout, Nashville Predators, separates them into two categories: those who are puck rushers and those who are not. The difference between a puck-rushing and puck-moving defenceman is pretty simple, and each organization and scout has their own preference. A puck mover has the ability to read the developing play and pass the puck to the correct option immediately to keep the play moving up the ice, while a puck rusher prefers to carry the puck and lead the play up the ice, becoming a fourth forward on the offensive attack.

"I put the defencemen into two different categories: one who takes the puck out of his zone, gets to the red line, and dumps it in, or you have your puck rushers who want to get up the ice into the offensive zone and create offense and try to make a play. As a scout, you can quickly tell which one is which, especially the ones that are desperate to get rid of the puck and don't look at any options, they just dump the puck in and don't join the rush."

"Now saying that, defencemen can be put into different situations where coaches tell them not to do certain things and some guys will get the green light to go. The next step is to see which defencemen are processing as they are moving

with the puck up the ice and if the puck is out in front of them and they are ready to make a pass or to stickhandle."

Knickle looks for defensive prospects who are fearless with the puck, but thinks finding them is tough.

"The biggest thing for me, and it hits me right in the face, is the guys that are not afraid to have the puck on their stick. If they do it, they are going to get better at it the more they handle it, so it goes hand in hand. Guys that are offensive minded, even if I have not seen them before, really stick out and they want to be that fourth forward. They don't just want to be a defensive defenceman and be able to bring offense from the back end. In the end, if you are not a puck rusher, I want you to be a good puck mover. Most guys are puck movers not puck rushers, and very few are like Scott Niedermayer or Mike Green."

The defenceman's hands and upper body movement are also important to *Knickle.*

"I look at a defenceman's hands on their stick and the rigidness of their shoulders, arms, and hands. It all correlates as the puck must be played from every position, even more than with forwards. If I see a defenceman with hands, then I am betting my bottom dollar that they know they have good hands and they are not afraid to handle the puck and want to handle the puck. For me, if I was going to put a finger on it, it was when I saw Cody Franson for the first time. So what did I see? Well, I saw a guy with calm hands who really did not feel like the pressure was on him."

Determining if a prospect is faster through the puck or their feet is an intricate but important aspect for *Tim Burke*. When play is faster through the puck, the puck moves faster than a player can skate. The play moves up the ice more quickly if a player, particularly a defenceman, can make a pass to a forward with speed. A defenceman who carries the puck out of the defensive zone himself takes more time than if he passes the puck, therefore he forces his forwards to slow down at the opposition's blue line. Having speed through the puck is important for defencemen, but finding it is rare. The difficulty of projecting this is one of the reasons why many scouts think defencemen are harder to scout than forwards.

"The determining factor is—is he faster through the puck or through his feet? And if he is faster through his feet, he has to be better skilled. Both Nick Lidstrom along with Zubov are perfect examples where the game is fast through the puck and they are not moving a lot. The game is quick because the puck is zipping around, so having the ability of having speed through the puck is more important than speed through your feet."

Skating

A defensive prospect's skating ability is another key thing that scouts must project. In addition to pivoting and skating backwards, defencemen are also asked to move laterally while skating backwards, something forwards rarely do. *Marty Stein* points out that defencemen have such a small margin for error when defending that every aspect of their skating must be examined.

"Some of the clues we look for in defencemen are balance, can he move laterally to get over to take a player out of the play, and does he have the turn catch-up speed? These are advantages we look for."

The ability to handle the variety of situations defencemen will encounter can come down to how effectively they skate, according to *Jay Heinbuck*.

"For defencemen, we look at their footwork and their edges and whether they can improve their agility, and a lot of improving agility comes with putting in the practice."

Heinbuck likes to examine the ability to pivot and turn, because this is something that defencemen must perform on every shift.

"What I look at mechanically is sometimes when a defence-man has to pivot and turn and go and retrieve a puck, what I call a Mohawk turn. Sometimes defencemen at this age group are in the habit of crossing over, but they should not cross over. I am as concerned about that as whether the defenceman has good balance and some fast twitch muscle fibre to work with, because you can only improve so much."

Offense

Defencemen are not generally expected to provide goal scoring on a regular basis. However, scouts must still try to access their ability to shoot. Since a defenceman shooting from the blue line is at a disadvantage due to the distance from the net, the accuracy and power of his shot become more of a factor than with a forward's shot.

> *"I look for a guy with his head up, that has some variety on his shots, and a little variety of their movement along the blue line. I was watching Nick Lidstrom the other day, and he doesn't shoot the puck 100 miles per hour but he drags the puck along the blue line with his stick, waiting for the forward to commit so then he can shoot and get the puck on net. I would rather have a defenceman place the puck on net in a certain area than blast it wide. As goalie, I hated when guys just placed it on net."*
>
> Rick Knickle

The Predators' own farm system provides *Knickle* with a good example of offensive defenders.

> *"Shea Weber's shot, nobody is tipping and everyone is parting like the Red Sea to get out of the way, so it is a different ball game, and the Al MacInnies, Sheldon Sourays are the far extreme. I like guys like Mike Green or Cody Franson that place pucks, and I want a guy more like that. We've got guys just like that in Jonathon Blum, who does not shoot the puck hard. I saw him with Milwaukee and he scored two goals and neither one of them dinted the back of the net."*

And finally, when trying to evaluate an offensive defenceman, *Rick Knickle* also thinks it's imperative to know a player's panic threshold with the puck. Defencemen with the puck face a different type and amount of pressure than a forward, making scouting offensive defencemen tougher than scouting offensive forwards.

> *"I think, for me, when I watch defencemen from an offensive perspective ... I want to see their panic threshold when they have the puck ... with nobody around them to begin with, and then, as he goes along, to see when he is pressured and how does he handles it when players are on him. And does he panic and make a play? Does he really not look comfortable and is he just getting rid of the puck? Especially defencemen, they are going to get far more pressure as they go along in their careers than forwards."*

SCOUTING FORWARDS

Now, not all scouts believe that defencemen are significantly more challenging to project. In fact, forwards have more styles, which can complicate matters as wingers must be evaluated differently than centres. *Jim Hammett* points out that determining whether a skilled forward can translate his skill to the NHL is a daunting task for all scouts. What compounds the projection issue is trying to determine if they have the intangibles to play another role at the NHL level.

> *"Yes, I do think it is more difficult to project certain player styles over others, and that is where you have to use your projection. Sometimes when you see a grinding player and you know he is going to be an up-and-down-his-wing type guy and a defensive player, I think that might be the ceiling for the player. But when you are projecting a skilled guy, you have to determine whether he is going to be a skilled*

*enough guy that can play on your top six or whether he can
be adaptable enough to play in your bottom six. So, I think
projecting a skilled player is a lot harder."*

Jim Nill thinks a playmaking forward can be the toughest
to scout. He points out that the hockey sense of the playmaker
is a key attribute that can make the difference between an
NHL star and career minor leaguer, but it is hard to define. He
admits scouts can miss it easily as they can get distracted by
other faults and lose sight of the big picture.

*"One thing I learned is if a forward has great hockey sense
and is not a great skater, the guy with hockey sense can
make up for it. There are great examples in the league. You
have Paul Stastny from Colorado—when he played in the
USHL and then college, we all knocked his skating. But
he has superior hockey sense and that transferred into him
being a star for Colorado. If you can find a player with
hockey sense, he is going to find a way to play even though
his skating might be off. That hockey sense is the diamond
in the rough."*

In addition, even scouts can get lured in by the attraction
of a scoring sensation in the junior ranks. But their success
can be misleading, and *Scott Luce* has seen many former sharp-
shooters forced to adapt to a checking role in order to achieve
NHL success.

*"Lots of prospects at the forward position that are phe-
nomenal scorers in junior or college end up being very good*

third- and fourth-line players in the NHL. Their success offensively just does not translate."

Ross Mahoney points out that there are countless talented offensive forwards in junior hockey who could not crack the top two lines in the NHL. This is one of the challenges scouts face when specifically scouting forwards. Figuring out if a point-producing junior forward can play a different role in the NHL and still contribute some offense is key for scouts. This is different than a forward accepting a different role on team, as the scouts must first project if the player can fulfill that role. It's great if a forward is willing to accept a different role, however, if he's unable to perform, his willingness becomes a moot point.

> *"One thing you have to keep in mind when you look at some of the checkers in the NHL is that if you go back, they probably were not checkers in junior hockey. I don't think people realize how talented you have to be as a player to be in the top two lines in the NHL. There are third- and fourth-line players in the NHL who, while in junior when they were 19 years old, had 100 points in a season and were among the top scorers of their leagues. But because they were smart and had skill, they could adapt to become good penalty killers and role players."*

Mark Kelley also looks for talented players with the willingness to accept roles and fit into a team.

> *"I think the easiest thing is when we are scouting them among their peers. Even when we are projecting them as*

role players they have a certain amount of skill. So even if we see a kid playing in junior scoring 30 goals, when we project them we realize that they scored 30 goals at that level. But going down the road we are projecting them to be a third-line- or fourth-line-type role player and what becomes important is a player's hockey sense and his ability to understand where he fits into a team concept."

Watching forwards play with Team Canada at tournaments is a great way to get more information on how they fulfill different roles.

"It's always good to go watch forwards play for Team Canada because they understand before they even get there that they are expected to be put into a role. It allows us to gauge how well they can play that role. Also, a lot of times when Team Canada are picking a team, they pick players based on what role they think that they can play and that gives us great insight."

Mark Kelley

Jim Nill points out that finding an elite offensive forward whose skill will translate to the NHL is tough.

"When you build your team there are only so many guys that are going to play on the power play and perhaps be top goal scorers. The key is to find a guy with skills, but you have to understand that the player's scoring prowess in junior will not translate to the NHL. A 10- or 20-goal scorer in junior might score 10 or 15 goals in the NHL, but 99 percent of the time it does not happen. It's finding

those forwards in the third or fourth round that have a good enough skill set to play in the NHL and hoping he is 6-foot-2 or 6-foot-3 and can also grind it out."

SCOUTING SCORECARD

Defencemen

- ❑ Can he be versatile and does he have good hockey sense?
- ❑ Is he quick through the puck?
- ❑ Is he a puck rusher or a puck mover?
- ❑ Does he have the skating ability?

Forwards

- ❑ Will the prospect be able to switch from a scorer to a checker?
- ❑ Does he have the willingness to change his role?
- ❑ Does he have good vision?
- ❑ Does he exhibit good hockey sense?

CHAPTER 15

The Intangibles

"I don't think scouts know whether the kid is going to be a leader or wants to be a leader until he is maybe 23 or 24."

Tim Burke, Director of Scouting, San Jose Sharks

The term "intangibles" gets thrown around all the time in hockey, but what does it mean from a scout's perspective? When they evaluate a prospect's intangibles, scouts are primarily trying to get a sense of the player as a person. To determine his character, they examine things other than his visible, on-ice skills. Each person evaluating these intangible characteristics comes with a different value system and an appreciation for certain qualities; however, regardless of each scout's personal bias there are consistent patterns that are prevalent in players who have had success in the NHL.

What a prospect does and says has a direct effect on whether or not they are considered to have legitimate NHL potential. First impressions come from brief chats with scouts following games. Scouts then spend time doing background research: watching video clips of interviews players have given and interviewing coaches and people who play a supporting role in the prospect's life (parents, billets, trainers, and so on). If prospects pass these initial investigations, they usually go on to have player meetings with any NHL team that is seriously considering drafting them. These meetings allow the player and the team to get to know each other better. Teams work hard to create a relaxed atmosphere that is more like a chat then a regular job interview because this gives them a greater chance to glimpse a player's true personality. (For a real-life example of what happens in a player meeting, please refer to Chapter 16).

LEADERSHIP

Leadership is often the first intangible quality that NHL scouts look for in prospects. Leadership involves demonstration of a strong work ethic in practices and games and dedication to nutrition and physical training. In addition, how a player communicates with his teammates and his willingness to mentor younger players is something scouts certainly consider. *Rick Dudley* points out the dramatic impact that good leadership can have on the success of an organization:

> *"I have been lucky enough to bring Dave Andreychuk to Tampa Bay and to watch his leadership and the way he*

impacted teammates. The things he said and did certainly brought that team a Stanley Cup for sure."

Craig Button believes that leaders are made, not born. Exposure to good role models and dedication to a certain level of behaviour creates good leadership skills. He offers the Kamloops Blazers of the WHL as an example of a team that created good leaders.

"I go back to Kamloops through Ken Hitchcock, Tom Renney, and Don Hay over that period of about 15 years. The young players had mentors and people to look up to, and when they became older they understood what leadership was. There wasn't just one leader or five leaders in Kamloops, they all understood leadership and they all took a leadership role. It was something that was valued by the Kamloops Blazers organization, and when you value it and help your players learn leadership, they will be better at it."

It can be difficult to assess leadership because of the prospects' youth, and scouts must take the teenagers' lack of maturity into account when projecting their abilities. *Button* references two of today's best-known players as examples:

"Did anyone think that some of the things that Sidney Crosby or Alexander Ovechkin did at 18 looked like what leaders in the NHL would do? When they were on the ice and they were losing, the answer would be no! But they were under a lot of pressure, and now that they're 23 and 25, that maturity and leadership has developed."

Even so, *Tim Burke* believes that the younger generations are benefitting from supportive environments and are learning to be leaders at a much younger age. However, being referred to as a great leader before stepping on NHL ice does not automatically make them great leaders at the NHL level; it just means they have the potential. After all, they are still rookies and need the guidance of NHL veterans.

> *"I remember when Kirk Muller was captain at a young age, and he worked his butt off while still trying to find his own niche in the NHL. It was a struggle every night, and to say he was going to lead some of the older guys was unfair, he needed some help from the older guys sometimes."*

It's important to balance a player's history with his current playing environment when determining his leadership potential. Sometimes a prospect is property of an organization that doesn't nurture leadership or that lacks leadership from management or coaching staff. *Button* notes:

> *"Of course you can go back over a player's history and look at whether he was a leader on his bantam team or midget team and ask different questions. A big part of it is what has their environment been like, and some players who were the captain on their bantam team suddenly end up in a bad situation in junior. Then someone says, 'They aren't a leader.' Well, how are they not a leader when they were the captain of their bantam, peewee, or midget team?"*

Jay Heinbuck cautions against taking the easy road and automatically flagging assistants or captains as leaders, as

wearing an *A* or a *C* on a sweater is not always an indicator of leadership in the future. He believes how a player
conducts himself on the ice is a more important indicator of
his potential to become an NHL-level leader.

*"With leadership it can seem as easy as, the player has a
letter on his jersey, but that is not always the case. Is the
prospect going out on the ice and giving more effort than
everyone else and leading by example? If you can't visibly
see it on the ice, then a scout must do his due diligence."*

Tim Burke agrees, and thinks that the most successful organizations are the ones that encourage leadership throughout
their rosters. He points out that even lower-level players can
still play an important leadership role on a team.

*"You see them develop into the sixth defenceman or a
fourth-line forward and think, 'How much can they lead
by example?' But that doesn't mean that he can't help in
the leadership group from within his role and by having a
good work ethic. I think Nick Lidstrom said it well, 'They
will listen when you have already backed it up.' Everybody
knows if you are pulling your weight."*

Leadership is an incredibly important quality for NHL
teams. Because exceptional captains in the NHL are few and far
between, prospects who show leadership potential are coveted
by scouts.

*"If you look around the NHL, out of the 30 teams, would
you say there are more than 10 leaders about whom you*

would say, 'Wow, he is an unbelievable captain'? You have to measure them against the Mark Messiers of the world."

Tim Burke

ICE TIME

Keeping track of a prospect's ice time can be a great tool for understanding his current ability to handle important situations. If a player is on one of the power play or penalty units, it may give some insight into which skills he excels at. Additionally, scouts need to watch which forwards are out on the power play when the team is down a goal on the road and which defencemen hit the ice in the last minute of the game to protect a one-goal lead. These are important clues that they use to identify the prospects who have the on-ice skills and the ability to handle pressure situations, and who are trusted by their coaches. This is even more significant in a prospect's NHL draft year, when coaching staff could rely on older, more mature junior or college players instead of the young prospects. This is information *Craig Button* uses regularly to round out a scouting report.

> *"The way I look at it, and always have, is the coaches have a great desire to win and they are going to play the players that are going to help them win. I think how they use players gives you as a scout really strong signals of what they think of players."*

He does point out that just seeing those situations is only the first part of that equation; understanding the coaches' rationale is equally important.

"But saying that, there must be a follow-up to that to ask the coaches, 'What do you think?' You need to find out why they used him there."

E.J. McGuire thinks noticing who the coaches put on the ice in certain critical situations is such a valuable tool for scouts that using the information is almost like cheating.

"When I say cheat, we do rely on the coaches. If we are looking for a centreman, is that the person, from the coach's vast knowledge of the player, who should be on the ice? Is this the player that he selects to take that final face-off or who he puts in the offensive zone when his team needs a goal or who he uses with six seconds left in any period in a defensive zone face-off?"

Sometimes a player isn't given enough credit for his ice time. Harkie Singh feels it's important to understand not just totals, but also when and where a player gets his ice time and when he is most productive.

"An example was Devin Setoguchi in his draft year. In Saskatoon, people were knocking him, saying that he doesn't compete with all the ice time he is given. Well, how can that be said when he scored the majority of his goals on the road, especially after multiple games in a row?"

"I look at how a guy plays after three games in four nights after travelling, because it only gets harder in the pro ranks and it gives you a hint of their intangibles. I used Setoguchi

as an example because when you break down stats and you look at where the production comes from, it's easier to play at home."

COMMUNICATION AND BODY LANGUAGE

Communication and body language are key indicators of whether a prospect will be a good teammate and has the proper attitude. Many times you will see scouts sit on the side opposite the players' benches so they can watch the players' reactions coming to and from the bench. *Rick Dudley* does this because he thinks an important measure of the prospect's character and maturity level is how he handles adversity.

"If something goes wrong on the ice, as scouts we want to see: does a prospect talk to his linemates when he gets back to the bench or does he sit there as if nothing happened?"

During his search for strong character, *Dudley* also appreciates how well a prospect communicates with his teammates on the ice. This can demonstrate the prospect's desire to contribute to an effective team effort.

"Communication on the ice is one of the intangibles scouts look for. I saw a prospect recently, he was always talking in the correct manner to his teammates, in the defensive zone especially, which is a good sign."

Another aspect for scouts to consider is emotional control, which is often portrayed through body language. This is an area *Scott Bradley* looks at carefully, especially if the prospect is supposed to be a leader. It is important for scouts to determine if the player has the desire to win and wants people to take responsibility so that can happen or if he just blames others for a lack of success.

> *"A scout is looking for little things over the course of a game, which you can see by body language. If a player is slumping or yipping at his teammates on the bench for a bad play, then maybe he's not the guy to lead the charge into battle. Some players take the bull by the horns and talk to their teammates and go out on the ice and show it. It's about doing it on the ice and showing by example."*

If you're looking for an example, *Harkie Singh* cites Edmonton Oilers draft pick Jordan Eberle as a good communicator with relaxed body language.

> *"A prospect like Jordan Eberle is poised and relaxed in all situations, and you can see that in his body language."*

OFF-ICE INTANGIBLES

Perhaps the intangible that gets the most discussion among the media and fans is a prospect's life away from the ice. When you are talking about 17- or 18-year-old kids who have had tremendous support systems in place, it takes scouts time to peel back the layers to get to the true character of a player. This is where scouts get to play Columbo or Sam Spade and do a little detective work. The scouts try to discover any bad habits that may have an adverse effect on the player's future team, such as consistent illicit drug use, uncontrolled gambling, or poor social manners. Manners may not seem like a big issue, but if a player routinely treats the people around him poorly, it could create problems for an NHL organization.

Sometimes pundits have unrealistic expectations about the behaviour and maturity level of prospects and forget what it's like to be that age. Certainly in today's era of mass media and instant access to information, prospects are under more pressure than ever before and should be given some leeway. *Tim Burke* agrees and he emphasizes how young and immature the prospects are when they're drafted.

> *"I think talking to as many people as possible, from different circumstances, about the player's background certainly helps. You can look at football as a comparison, where they are drafted into the NFL at 21 or 22, after three or four hard years of college football. They have a greater maturity level compared to hockey."*

He stresses the importance of speaking with as many people as possible to obtain different perspectives on the prospect, particularly as a prospect can get a bad reputation from one source that spreads, even if it isn't justified.

> *"Sometimes players get railroaded early on, with one coach saying he isn't a great kid, and then four years later everyone says he is a leader."*

A little piece of information like that can circulate among the scouts and media alike and take on a life of its own. A tremendous amount of due diligence is required to separate fact from fiction. *Jay Heinbuck* makes sure his scouts are resourceful and cautious when investigating rumours.

"We ask our scouts to do that type of background work. It's funny, as you know, hockey is a small world. You start to hear a lot of things about the prospects, especially if it's negative and the rumour mills are out there. If you do hear something negative, then you have to start asking coaches and others to dig up the truth."

Another reason that scouts must dig deeper than in the past is due to the number of people directly involved with the prospects. Scouts must navigate through all the information they obtain and determine the motivation of the person who provided it before deciding if that player is right for them. *Gordie Clark* corroborates this and thinks scouts in the industry all have to do more investigating.

"We have to do way more background work than ever before because there so many more reasons involved. With agents and parents so involved with their kids' careers because the money is so big, it's big decisions and big money involved, and you have to do way more homework."

Certainly this background work on a prospect can produce red flags. *Rick Dudley* has had situations where a prospect's character dictated where he was chosen in the draft.

"It has happened a few times where I have done an investigation on a player that probably dropped him down. It didn't eliminate him from being drafted, but if you are

building a team based on character and you find something that shows a lack of character, then you probably stay away from someone like that."

Once the detective work is done and the scouts have established what is true and what is merely gossip, *Craig Button* cautions against overanalyzing the information.

"You have to speak with people that are with a player on a daily basis, and that could be teachers and billets and coaches. Look at their information along with how receptive is he to being coached, and that starts putting the pieces together. Do the research to understand what type of person you have and how open they are, and it's not any more complicated than that!"

SCOUTING SCORECARD

❑ Does the prospect show leadership qualities, regardless of whether or not he wears an *A* or a *C* on his sweater?

❑ Does his coach reward him with lots of ice time?

❑ How is that ice time allocated: is he put out in clutch situations?

❑ Can he communicate effectively with his teammates on the ice and on the bench?

❑ Does he exhibit relaxed, confident body language?

❑ Does he show strength of character by behaving acceptably off the ice?

CHAPTER 16

An Inside Look at a Player Meeting

"In many situations, the scout just wants to sit down with the players and interview them. If you just let the prospect talk, it will reveal a lot about him."

Jeff Gorton, Assistant Director of Player Personnel,

New York Rangers

I was very fortunate that the San Jose Sharks allowed me to sit in on two of their prospect interviews prior to the 2010 NHL Draft. Most teams have an agenda detailing what type of questions will be asked of each prospect and why they are being asked. If an organization covets certain personality traits in a player, a specific line of questioning may be pursued to try to gauge if he has the desired characteristics. Keep in mind that each organization has a different style and asks questions in a different manner. To give you insight into the process, I'm providing some of the details of Kirill Kabanov's prospect interview with the Sharks.

In terms of skill and potential, Kabanov was considered a top-15 draft choice, but skill is not the only factor when a player is drafted. He had come under some scrutiny for off-ice incidents, and the Sharks, and many other teams, were wondering about his perspective on them. I'll provide you with a brief background, which will be helpful in setting the stage for the meeting.

Kabanov gained his playing freedom from the Kontinental Hockey League by appealing to the IIHF and came to play with the Moncton Wildcats of the Canadian Hockey League. Unfortunately, he suffered a wrist injury that curtailed his season. The Wildcats were very successful in his absence. When he returned from his injury, the highly skilled Kabanov wished to continue to play on the top two lines, where he had left off. Giving him the spot would have meant taking it away from someone who had earned it all year long. This caused a difficult situation. It was unfair to Kabanov to be denied his old spot simply due to an injury, but it was also unfair to the player who had successfully filled his spot while he was away. Since it was late in the season, with the playoffs looming, a decision was made to satisfy both parties: Head Coach Danny Flynn allowed Kabanov to return to Russia to play for his homeland in the spring U18 tournament.

Everything seemed fine until Kabanov was removed from the Russian team under unclear circumstances and subsequently banned from playing in the KHL and internationally for Russia for a set period of time. NHL teams were unsure what had transpired. Was this just a way for the Russians to send future prospects a message that if they dare defy the KHL by leaving, there will be ramifications, or was this a prima donna player not getting what he wanted and the Russian management taking issue with his behaviour? Further muddying the waters was the fact that Kabanov changed player agents twice since becoming draft eligible, which always raises eyebrows amongst the scouts. Needless to say, NHL teams were keen to speak to this young man before heading into the Draft.

With great anticipation, I sat waiting for Kabanov with the San Jose Sharks scouting staff, including Director of Scouting Tim Burke, Gilles Cote, Pat Funk, Jack Gardiner, Rob Grillo, Brian Gross, Shinn Larson, Bryan Marchment, Karel Masopust, Joe Will, and General Manager Doug Wilson. Kabanov gave a good first impression when he walked into the room. He came with a genuine smile on his face and made the first move to introduce himself and shake everyone's hand. This was a smart move, as it set the mood and made everyone in the room feel at ease. Once Kabanov sat down, he seemed confident, comfortable, and genuine.

Since the Sharks had already spoken to Kabanov at the NHL combine, the majority of the meeting was a follow-up. Once everyone got situated, Tim Burke opened the questions in a casual manner, asking about Kabanov's flight from Moscow and how he liked Los Angeles. The discussion quickly turned to the World Cup and the fact Russia was not there.

Tim Burke asked Kabanov, *"What's wrong with Russian foot-ball?"* With a roll of his eyes and a shrug of his shoulders, Kabanov responded, *"I do not know,"* in a tone of disgust. He pointed out that perhaps they were overconfident and didn't take their competition, like Slovenia, seriously enough. Tim Burke said, *"You don't have a problem with confidence,"* and Kabanov just smiled and said, *"No! No problems."* Then Kabanov asked Tim Burke about the USA-Ghana game. Tim Burke responded, *"I'm nervous about the game,"* and Pat Funk and Brian Gross piped up with, *"What are you talking about? You don't even like soccer,"* and everyone laughed.

With the ice broken, Tim Burke asked if any veteran Russian NHLers had told him how tough it would be training for the NHL game. He said, *"Yeah, Branko Radivojevich,"* which gave us all a laugh since he happens to not be Russian. Kabanov laughingly commented that, *"The training was very hard, almost as tough as Russia."* Then Burke asked him if there were any NHLers from Kabanov's hometown, to which Kabanov replied, *"Yes, Ovechkin."* Burke asked, *"Is he a little crazy?"* to which he replied, *"No, Radulov,"* prompting more laughter from the group. Burke noted, *"He loves the fans,"* but Kabanov quickly corrected him with a Cheshire-cat smile, *"No, he likes the girls and the vodka."*

Then Kabanov made an amusing observation about how people drank in Moncton compared to Moscow. *"In Russia, we eat when we drink vodka, but in Moncton, they just drink, and that is why we drink more."* This opened up the line of questioning so the guys could try to get a sense of Kabanov's perspective of what happened at the end of his season in Moncton and to determine if there were any hard feelings. The first thing mentioned was that Bryan Marchment had lived in Moncton, which made Kabanov sit up a little straighter in his chair. Then Burke said, *"Do you know what I say about Moncton? It's the best place to stay for two days."* Somewhat defensively, Kabanov asked why, as if he couldn't believe anyone would dare to say something bad about Moncton. Burkie relaxed him by saying, *"You get a lobster, a French woman, and then get out of town."* *"How about the rink in Moncton?"* asked Brian Gross. Kabanov replied, *"It is a great rink,"* and Burkie added, *"How about the French women?"* Kabanov smiled a little and said, *"They are good, but I like Russian women better!"*

The subject changed to Kabanov's style of game as Tim Burke asked him to describe the best part of his game to the guys in the meeting who had not seen him play. In an almost apologetic manner, he shrugged and said, *"A playmaker, handling the puck and making passes, and on the power play."* Then Rob Grillo added, *"So, you're more of a playmaker than a goal scorer?"* Kabanov replied in an almost uncomfortable stammer, *"I like to get assists,"* almost as if he didn't want to admit it.

His mood improved when Tim Burke told him, *"You are a dangerous player!"* Kabanov quickly said, *"Yes,"* with a big smile. Then as a pronouncement to us in the room, Burke added, *"He's always dangerous and can make things happen when he has the puck."* To follow up, Burke asked what type of player he likes to play with on his line. Kabanov replied, *"Aggressive."* When Tim probed further as to the exact type and brought up Nick Backstrom from Washington, Kabanov said, *"No, I like more Russian."* *"How about the Czech players?"* Burke asked, smiling at Czech scout Karel Masopust, knowing the hockey history between the two nations. Kabanov shrugged and said, *"They are okay to play with."* Then Burke leaned forward in his chair and said, *"Canadians,"* trying to find someone the kid likes to play with. Surprisingly, Kabanov replied with a huge smile, like you were talking about old friends, *"Yes, they are great to play with."* Burke said, *"So, you want a big strong guy and somebody that shoots the puck?"* *"That works for me!"* answered Kabanov.

Then Rob Grillo changed into a more serious tone and asked Kabanov *"How did the NHL combine go for you?"* Kabanov made some guys chuckle by dismissing the difficulty level of the tests, except for the bench press, which he admitted he did not practise. Then Tim Burke inquired about the injuries that Kabanov suffered, but he assured us he was fine, although he admitted he was tired after the flight from Moscow.

When the discussion turned to training over the summer, he pointed out that he would be going back to Moscow for some specialized training for a while and then joining Bobby Orr's hockey camp in August. Pat Funk asked, *"Will all his players be there?"* Kabanov confirmed this, which seemed to satisfy the scouts. Then Burke asked if Kabanov was going to return to Russia after that, but he said, *"I am staying in North America."* Burke added, *"So you will go to an NHL camp?"* and Kabanov replied, *"Yes, that is right,"* with confidence.

In a stern voice, Tim Burke said to Kabanov, *"You have to be ready for an NHL training camp. It's tough and a lot of guys are fighting for a job, and they are fast, big, and strong. Are you sure you are going to be ready?"* With a cocky nod of his head, he indicated that he would be ready if San Jose drafted him.

Talk moved over to Dan Flynn, who was Kabanov's coach in Moncton, and Burke asked if Kabanov had talked to him lately. *"Yes, I talked to him yesterday, and he is here at the Draft,"* said Kabanov, and Bryan Marchment piped in, *"He coached me as well."* It's not only the answers, but also the body language that gives the scouts a true idea of what a player thinks of his coach. In a genuinely respectful way, Kabanov said, *"He is a really good guy."* Then he asked Marchment, *"He was your assistant coach?"* and Bryan clarified, *"No, he was my head coach in Belleville."* Kabanov added, *"Wow, he is old,"* which made the rest of us smile.

After some more small talk about Moncton, Tim Burke inquired if his family had come over and if they were excited. Then he asked who was the boss of the family. Kabanov's smartass response was, *"Well, me."* But then he admitted his mother was in charge. Burke added, *"When the mother is the boss, there are fewer problems,"* and Kabanov noted, *"She is pretty tough,"* with a seriously worried look on his face, which made everyone laugh. This prompted Kabanov to say, *"My Dad is pretty big, so if my Mom has problem, she just has to say something to him. Then there are no problems!"* and all the scouts laughed harder.

"We need more right-handed goal scorers on our team," Burke said to Kabanov, as he is a right-handed shot. Then Burke and the guys make reference to players like Mike Bossy, Mario Lemieux, Steve Yzerman, and Stan Mikita, who were all right-handed shots. As Burke pointed out the advantage of being

a right-handed shot, Kabanov jumped in and agreed and finished Burke's sentence for him.

Since the meeting seemed to be coming to a close, Burke got down to brass tacks and asked Kabanov what his expectations were for next season. Without a hesitation, Kabanov replied, *"Work hard in the off-season and try to make the NHL, and if not, whatever the NHL team that drafts me wants me to do I will do, and if the NHL team wants me to go to junior that is where I will go."* Burkie flipped it back on Kabanov, *"Well, where will that be?"* With a confused look, Kabanov said, *"In Moncton."* Burkie followed up by saying, *"Well, Danny Flynn wants you back and they need scoring, so Moncton should be a good fit."* They talked about the few older guys on Moncton who would be leaving and whether Kabanov thought Brandon Gormley would be back.

Then there was a pause in the banter, it seemed as if everyone in the room took a big collective breath. This gave Burke a chance to say, *"Well, you seem prepared and have a plan for the summer,"* to which Kabanov responded, *"If you draft me, I will not disappoint you."* Burke brought up the fact it's a big year for Kabanov and that the WJC was being held in Buffalo. However, Kabanov said, *"I do not care, I am done with Russian National Team."* Pat Funk and Brian Gross both confirmed that Kabanov had said the same thing to them at the NHL combine. Burke wanted to know, *"What if the National Team wants your scoring?"* But Kabanov was firm.

As the meeting ended, Tim Burke made mention of Kabanov's talent and his potential to have a good season and thanked him for meeting with the rest of the staff. He made a point of saying to Kabanov, *"You seem like a good teammate, and you are a lot of fun and happy."* Then the scouts stood up and shook Kabanov's hand and thanked him for meeting with them. After reading all the reports on him and meeting him a couple of times, it was easy to see how likeable the kid is.

The San Jose Sharks did not end up drafting Kirill Kabanov, but he was selected in the third round by the New York Islanders, 65th overall.

Some people wonder why NHL scouting staffs have these meetings in the first place, when all they have to do is read the player's psychology report. These meeting are valuable for scouting departments because they provide an opportunity to see some of the prospect's personality, intelligence, and character. They also can be used to find out if all the information scouts have collected over the year was accurate and if not, the player can fill in any holes. Additionally, some teams think that a kid can bullshit a psychology test but not a room full of experienced scouts. While prospects may understandably be nervous prior to these meetings, you can see from the example above that they are low-key affairs. The team is genuinely trying to get a read on the player as a person and is not going to serve up any trick questions, as might happen in a regular job interview.

APPENDIX

Player Development

"I think it's important to keep in context the current age and place in which they are playing. Understand that a 20-year-old is just that, he's a 20-year-old, and each individual has different maturation processes and timelines that they go through. As much as we as an organization may have a certain timeline, the players as individuals have their own, and I think it's very critical to take each individual case by case."

Craig Billington, Assistant General Manager,
Colorado Avalanche

Although player development is not the primary concern of scouts, their observations are essential in building a successful prospect development program. Developing prospects has become much more important and has been given a higher profile within NHL organizations since the new CBA, which makes less expensive players more valuable. NHL organizations have, for the most part, locked up their core players to high-salary long-term contracts. Due to the salary cap, younger, cheaper players are squeezing out the higher-priced veteran role players who previously dominated the third and fourth lines and the fifth to seventh defenceman spots. This puts a tremendous strain on scouting and player development staff to find players who can almost immediately make the jump out of junior or college. This strategy of bringing prospects in quickly can often backfire, as the majority of young players are not mentally or emotionally ready to handle the stress of playing in the NHL.

The NHL teams have been clambering over themselves to hire player development staff who can mould the young prospects into masterpieces. The new environment has fostered an entire new industry inside of hockey, which is starting to pay dividends for the game itself. When prospects are given the time to develop their games and also to mature as individuals, it allows them to have a greater focus on the game itself. That's why the American Hockey League is such a crucial step in a prospect's development process. The AHL allows prospects to learn to be a professional on and off the ice in a more controlled environment, with a few more checks and balances than in the NHL.

Some NHL organizations have had player development staffs for longer than others and are currently ahead of the curve. Two prime examples of organizations that do a consistently good job in slowly developing their players are the Detroit Red Wings and the San Jose Sharks. Both refuse to jeopardize the development of their prospects by forcing them into on- and off-ice situations that will cause them to fail. That is a difficult balance for NHL organizations to find, as the pressure to win *now* is enormous, often at the expense of developing players for the future. But all NHL teams and owners have begun to realize that spending an extra million dollars on a free agent contract is wasteful; it doesn't have the same impact on the long-term success of the team as hiring a player development staff for similar money.

PLAYER DEVELOPMENT STAFF

NHL player development staffs can involve skating coaches, puck-skills coaches, goalie coaches, conditioning coaches, nutritionists, and psychologists. This group works with the prospects in their organizations to prepare them to potentially play in the NHL. Once a prospect has been drafted or signed as a free agent, the information gathered by the scouts will go to the player development department. NHL development staff assess the prospects they currently have in their system and make a development plan specifically for them. These programs start in the summer, when prospects attend a prospect camp where the entire development staff can get an honest assessment of where they currently are in their development and what has to be worked on in the future. The work does not end there for the staff, as they will often travel to monitor progress and work with prospects throughout the season. The development staff also will work with the prospects who are currently playing in their farm system in the AHL and the ones playing in the junior ranks across North America and Europe.

Trevor Timmins thinks that as they continue to evolve they'll grow to address even more specific issues, such as one-on-one battles, positioning, and puck protection.

The new-found co-operation of the junior hockey teams has contributed to the more rapid development of players. Junior hockey organizations have recently changed their philosophies and agreed to let outside personnel have access to their players, which is crucial to long-term success. *Paul Castron*, Director of Player Personnel, Columbus Blue Jackets, has received positive feedback and finds the players are benefitting from hearing another perspective.

"The junior teams are really receptive to it. Many times they are trying to get through to their players. If they hear the same message from another voice, then maybe they understand that it's not, 'My coach is picking on me.'"

One of the challenges that player development staff face is lack of willingness in some prospects. While they have to take into account that many of these prospects are still young—17, 18, and 19 years old—in some cases, it still frustrates them. *Paul Castron* notes that attitude is key for players who want to make it to the next level.

"Lower-round prospects might have a better chance to make it to the NHL through player development. They don't have as high an expectation of putting up points as you normally have when you take a forward in the first round. Sometimes the skilled player does not want to adapt, and they say, 'Well, I'm an offensive player and I'll get my 80 points in the minors.' The less skilled players will block shots and

sacrifice and find a way to make it. For example, we have a kid from out West, Derek Dorsett, and he is like, 'Nobody is going to deny me, and I will find a way to make it.' It's the common sense factor: do you want to make that sacrifice and commitment to make $500,000 or do you want to make $50,000 in the minors?''

When working with Europeans, player development staff must also take into account the cultural and stylistic differences that players will need to adapt to when they're being developed. *Craig Billington* points out some of the differences:

"There are so many factors in getting a European player to come over here, starting with the different minor hockey development programs. In addition to it being a different style of hockey, they might practise seven days a week but only play one game every two weeks. A major junior team over here might play three games in three nights. The Europeans might be playing three games in three weeks. How is the player going to hold up to the grind? There are a lot of intangibles that come into play.''

He thinks it's important for player development staff to help the prospects succeed by treating them as individuals and structuring programs on a case-by-case basis, taking into account their personality, characteristics, and maturity level.

THE ONE-WEEK PROSPECT CAMP

Trevor Timmins feels the starting point for player development departments was the creation of team summer development camps. Each NHL team organizes a training camp for its prospects to assess where they currently are in their development cycle. Unfortunately, due to a clause in the CBA, teams must limit these camps to seven days. Since the NHL teams only have a week with their prospects, they have to try to cram a year's worth of player development into seven days. This restriction may seem shortsighted, and it is. It was created in part to protect the lower-revenue NHL organizations that don't want to devote capital to player development. In addition, the National Hockey League Players' Association (NHLPA) felt that NHL teams should not be allowed to dictate the off-season activities of first-year professional players, for which they are not paid. This is slightly ridiculous because at that stage the prospects are not even members of the NHLPA yet. The most important asset the NHL has is the next generation of prospects, as they will determine the quality of play in the future NHL. Now, I'm not saying NHL teams should have prospects for the entire summer, but a one-week development camp is clearly not enough. This situation is not ideal, so staff must construct player development strategies for each prospect, which they then take back to their own specialty coaches and trainers and attempt to continue on their own.

"We don't get a lot of quality time to spend with our drafted prospects until they turn pro. Once they become a part of your franchise, whether it be in the minor league club or the NHL club, it's easier. So anytime you get a chance to work with these young players, the earlier the better."

Tom Kurvers

Paul Castron agrees that only having the prospects for one week of structured NHL-supervised development restricts the players' advancement. He thinks it would be worthwhile to spend additional funds to access the personnel resources needed to expand the development camps so they last longer. He points to how the National Football League structures their development camps and believes the NHL would benefit greatly from a similar philosophy. The more access and direct preparation each NHL team has with its prospects, the greater a chance the prospects have of playing in the NHL. Not only would the competition for jobs increase, but the skill level of the prospects would also improve, which would make for a more exciting product on the ice.

I think we are handicapped with only the one week in the summer when we can have our prospects. I think everyone agrees with that and feel it would help the development of the prospects if we had more freedom. Now, some teams didn't think it was fair because they did not want to spend the money. I was thinking, 'If it was $100,000 for the summer to house, feed, and train the kids, then what is that in the grand scheme of things?'

"I know teams have been reprimanded for doing prospect development outside of that one-week window, and it's almost like you have to. Say, for example, Steven Stamkos signs the day after he is drafted and he has all these bonuses that have to be paid out. The organization does not have the right to train him and get the value and their money's worth from their investment. The team hands him a bunch of money, but then has no say what he does in terms of training off the ice, and that is ridiculous. The NFL has all

their mini-camps all the time and if guys don't show up, they get fined, and they have access to them three to four times a year."

PHYSICAL DEVELOPMENT

Although specific physical training has been the norm in hockey for quite some time, there has been dramatic advancement over the past decade. The prospects are now employing personal trainers, sometimes on their own and sometimes at the request of the NHL teams that have drafted them. The young athletes are now exposed to an Olympic-style training regime coupled with nutritional expertise, which includes not only providing them with a diet to follow but also with the rationale behind the diet.

The level of competition has risen due directly to this training, as players with lesser skills can create a more level playing field with hard work. However, *Craig Billington* reminds us that each individual player's physical development is unique. The balance between sports-specific training and building a foundation for an underdeveloped player is a constant challenge.

"I think it's a process, a multi-layered process, and there is a lot of science behind it. Perhaps more importantly, there is a lot of want from the player behind it. You need to provide those environments that allow him to grow and mature and maximize his ability to reach his potential. I think Olympic athletes have been doing this forever, and I think in the hockey business we've gotten a lot better in the past decade at recognizing the importance of it and catering to those individuals, both in terms to their training on the

ice and off. It's the first step in a full scope of what I call 'the professional life.'"

LIFESTYLE COACHING

Sometimes we forget that parents, coaches, and billet families have insulated the majority of these young prospects. So these players have never done many of the day-to-day duties we take for granted. Simple things like doing laundry, buying groceries, and paying bills are things these kids have not had to do. Player development programs have made strides in addressing this issue. NHL teams recognize that these added stresses on a young prospect, especially when he just turns pro, could cause adverse effects on the ice. Teams also have programs in place to help players avoid some of the common pitfalls of having new-found personal and financial freedom. How many times have we seen young men with vast financial resources at their disposal make poor choices that in turn directly affect their hockey careers? The NHL teams have made a greater commitment to preparing these players and taking a one-on-one approach to prevent this from happening.

When *Craig Billington* made his way into player development after his playing days were over, he was surprised at the lack of discussion of these issues.

"It's interesting when you look at development 10 years ago; the odd word about it would come up, but there was not much lifestyle discussion. Now pretty much every team has got someone, or a department, that works with their kids, so it is really evolving. It has evolved and I believe

*will continue to. Like in life, one-on-one personal relations
are critical in order to have success."*

SOCIOLOGICAL COMMUNICATION

Further to lifestyle coaching, simply building a relationship
with the players is critical. All the science and technology
that goes into the physical training will be pointless if there
isn't mutual trust and understanding between the players
and the organization. The players need to trust the organization's decisions and understand the reasons for them while
the organization must learn to trust that the players will
give their very best effort and be open and honest in all
communications.

*"I think it's all part and parcel of building a trusting
relationship with that person. But like I said, there are all
different aspects to a situation and you must have intuition
and feel. A strong relationship with a player can enable you
to create a plan for that player that will allow him to have
the best success."*

Craig Billington

The key to the entire player development department is
not the plan, but the people responsible for the communication and implementation of the plan. Finding individuals
with the ability to listen to the players can make or break the
future of the organization.

*"I think having someone in the player development depart-
ment that is in touch with today's player and game is very*

important. Also, it's vital to relate to them, to put themselves in the players' shoes, and to be able to communicate with them. I think the communication skills are key to having success in the player development department. The people that can effectively communicate not only get their message listened to, but actually heard."

Craig Billington

PSYCHOLOGICAL TESTING

The psychological testing now provided by NHL teams certainly has some benefit, and each organization has its own criteria and standards, which they do not reveal publicly. Some of the testing provides a snapshot of the mental, emotional, and social strengths and weaknesses of each player. The testing and how a player views and reacts to different circumstances on and off the ice can provide some indication of whether or not he can fulfill his potential.

Former NHL scout and current sports psychologist *Paul Henry* gives some insight into his role and how crucial this area is to choosing and developing the right players. The advantage *Henry* has over other sports psychologists is his experience as a scout. This allows him a greater understanding of what the scouts have seen and what a prospect needs to develop.

"Similar to other sports psychologists, my expertise is helping the players flush out anxiety and to get them to see their feelings clearly. When they are seeing themselves clearly, they are more likely to build and continue with good habits in overall life. As a sport psychologist, I deal in feelings and

my basic tenet is that you have to feel good to play good,
and it's your responsibility as a player to bring excellence
to your dressing room every night."

Those are the types of things that sports psychologists focus on—they are in the business of helping players help themselves. Like many sports psychologists, *Paul Henry* helps players sort out their feelings, as there is a lot of anxiety in the hockey world. The players are anxious about new contracts and anxious to make sure they don't fail and let others down. It's that anxiety and the pressure these young prospects endure and how they deal with it that can affect their NHL potential.

"I have a tenet: anxiety destroys self-confidence, yet con-
versely, self-confidence destroys anxiety. It's a matter of
releasing the anxiety because the anxiety cripples and
destroys your ability to be as good as they know you can be.
That is why players are so hard on themselves when they're
not playing the way they can. Once they believe they are
in trouble, it can be a downward spiral, and players run
themselves out of the league, out of hockey."

According to *Henry*, NHL teams often miss a crucial step in the prospects' development by not putting greater resources into this area. He thinks many prospects fail to fulfill their potential because they lack emotional and mental skills.

"This is what can happen if prospects and their NHL orga-
nizations do not do anything for them from an emotional
or mental perspective. Every NHL organization spends a
ridiculous amount of money in the summertime building

their bodies up but not enough of them pay attention to developing their individual mental and emotional skills."

Craig Billington thinks it's important not to lose sight of the individual and what they bring to the mix. His experience in the locker room has taught him that regardless of what the tests say, the sum is more than the parts in individuals and teams.

"There are these different facets you can have in place, but never lose sight of what that person is as a player. I was fortunate to play for 18 years, and if I looked back on every roster I played on, there were a bunch of different characters supporting that team. It is important to keep that in mind and remember what the locker room mix is like, and it takes all kinds of personalities to make a team become a Stanley Cup success."

He also points out that an open mind is required, as the answers from clinical diagnoses may not give you the insight into a winning formula. In the past, *Billington* has witnessed players who may have been dismissed by some teams based on testing results, but who had other factors that made them successes.

"You can't get so focused that you have this textbook criteria with a checklist of all the things that the player has to be. I think you have to be open-minded and receptive, and there are a number of players I know that were very effective to the outcome of the team but who had been challenged in other areas."

Index